The

INTUITIVE
HEALER

The

INTUITIVE

HEALER

Accessing Your Inner Physician

MARCIA EMERY, PH.D.

Foreword by Caroline Myss, Ph.D.

St. Martin's Press ☁ New York

Grateful acknowledgment is given for permission to reprint an excerpt from *Our Dreaming Mind* by Robert L. Van de Castle, Ph.D. Copyright © 1995 by Robert L. Van de Castle, Ph.D. Reprinted by permission of Ballantine Books, a division of Random House, Inc. The prayer by Dr. Patrick Tribble is reprinted by permission of the author. The poem "You Are" by Margery Johnson is reprinted by permission of the author.

Design by Leah Carlson-Stanisic

Library of Congress Cataloging-in-Publication Data

Emery, Marcia.
    The intuitive healer : accessing your inner physician ; foreword by Caroline Myss.—1st ed.
        p.   cm.
    ISBN 0-312-19902-3
    1. Intuition.   2. Healing.   I. Title.
RZ999.E44   1999
615.5—dc21   98-11670
                                                        CIP

First Edition: March 1999

10   9   8   7   6   5   4   3   2   1

THIS BOOK IS DEDICATED TO

Mr. Lynn "Buck" Charlson,
a true visionary, who has generously supported my work
in the field of intuition over the past eight years.

CONTENTS

Contents

ACKNOWLEDGMENTS

T he process of writing a book, from its inception until the final
page, has many parallels with the birthing process. My gratitude
to everyone who helped "midwife" this book is expressed in the
following quote from Flavia.

*Some people come into our lives, make footprints on our heart,
and we are never the same.*

The people seen and unseen who helped me breathe life into and
create this book all left footprints on my heart. I acknowledge them
for their contributions throughout the gestation and birthing
process.

I honor the voice that speaks through me—the source of all life
who has many names and descriptions. For me, it is the godlike
energy, that still voice within, that inspired and truly created this
work.

Although my mother, Naomi Rose, is no longer on this earth
plane, her essence continually inspires me, as I still feel her pride in
my creative and communication skills. She is joined in the spheres
by my father, Dr. David Gelfand, favorite uncle, Dr. Louis Gelfand,
grandfather Paul Magnus, and father-in-law, Wendell Emery. I can
see their smiling faces as this book is presented to the world.

I am grateful to Candice Fuhrman for leading me to my literary agent, Bonnie Solow, and for providing invaluable input as this book was being created. I highly praise Bonnie for her extraordinary inner vision, which helped to elevate this book to the highest level.

This book has felt complete as a work of art thanks to the adept and skilled editing of Doug Childers, who amplified its brush strokes in an exceptional way.

To Heather Jackson, Rebecca Koh, and the staff at St. Martin's Press, I express my gratitude for recognizing the value of this work. My appreciation to Mary Marin for reading the preliminary drafts of this book.

My thanks to my dear friends who have supported my work in articulating intuition. They include Jeffrey Mishlove, Pete Raynolds, Colleen Mauro, Sharon Franquemont, Nancy Rosanoff, Roger Frantz, Barbara Schultz, Victor Beasley, Michele Grace, Karen Kramer, Janis Marshall, Lars Spivock, and the staff of the Life Science Foundation.

To my chiropractor, Patrick Tribble, who is a magnificent model of an intuitive healer.

And to my beloved husband, Jim, I want to give you the most priceless gem of all, my eternal gratitude for always being there to take care of me in many ways with your unending supply of love.

FOREWORD

W riting a book about intuition is not an easy task. In many ways, it's like writing about how air travels through cheesecloth—it's real, to be sure, but impossible to hold. Marcia Emery has succeeded in this sizable task, giving us a book on intuitive instruction that is both a pleasure to read and immensely useful.

In *The Intuitive Healer: Accessing Your Inner Physician*, Marcia fulfills her promise of taking us on a step-by-step guide into our own sensory system. She offers exercises that encourage us readers to articulate our strengths, our fears, and our blockages—all of which form the core toward helping us to know more about why it is we become ill.

I have always believed that we are intuitive by nature. Intuition is our most natural sense, even more than sight, touch, or hearing. In my own workshops on Intuitive Development, I went through a transition. During the early days when I first began teaching this subject, I felt obligated to produce some type of exercise that would guarantee that my students would be clear "intuitives" by the end of their week with me. But no matter what type of exercise I came up with, nothing seemed to provide full proof.

Then the light went on in my head. I realized that these individuals were coming to me not because they wanted to develop their intuition, but because their intuition was already incredibly well developed. What they did not recognize was that their doubt or confusion was, in fact, the energy of intuition urging them to make some new choices in their lives. These students, and many to follow, were under the mistaken impression that intuitive ability was the capacity to see the future so clearly that no errors would be made, particularly in the decision-making arenas of money, occupation, or romance. They believed that intuition was the ability to foresee and avoid pain, mistakes, or financial loss.

That is not intuitive ability. Intuition is the ability to interpret the energetic information that is always a part of every aspect of life and to use that energetic information for making wise choices—not safe, but wise. Intuition does not promise an end to all pain; in fact, pain and pleasure should not even factor into our understanding of intuition. Intuitive ability has much more to do with learning to rely upon our natural wisdom than it does with developing a means of protection. The very essence of the need to protect is fear, whereas wisdom is linked to the recognition that life is essentially a learning experience. As such, pain and pleasure are partners. To focus only on pleasure and safety is like desiring to live only in sunlight—an impossible goal.

No matter how much we focus our attention on attaining and maintaining health, we will each inevitably face challenges in this area. These challenges are simply a part of life. Thus, there is great wisdom in learning to respond to our innate intuitive sense that we are in a situation which is causing us to lose power. In paying attention, and in then making an appropriate decision to reverse the situation, we maximize our chances of remaining healthy and avoid having to become ill in order to learn that we do not want to be in certain toxic situations or relationships.

Of course, you must bear in mind that intuition requires personal courage in order to thrive. You cannot decide to be "conveniently" intuitive, incorporating only information that does not upset you or cause you to make any changes in your life. In developing this skill, you must be willing to honor it as a sight you will use without blinders. You cannot expect clarity on demand. The biggest block to intuitive development is the fear that comes with being clear-sighted, because clear-sightedness means that you must make clear choices. Choice means change, and change frightens people even more than dying.

Marcia's wonderful book can become a powerful tool. I encourage you to follow her exercises, doing each of them with a serious focus of mind and heart. Moreover, I would ask you to pay attention to your own fear of how your life would change were you to become a clear intuitive. In doing these exercises and paying attention, you will learn a great deal about your own comfort level with becoming a more intuitive individual. And last but not least, enjoy the journey through the pages of this book. I know I did.

—Caroline Myss, Ph.D., author of *Anatomy of the Spirit* and *Why People Don't Heal and How They Can*

INTRODUCTION

The history of science makes clear that the greatest advancements in man's understanding of the universe are made by intuitive leaps at the frontiers of knowledge, not by intellectual walks along well-traveled paths.
— ANDREW WEIL, *The Natural Mind*

I am lucky to have a special guide who alerts me to any impending health crisis. If I feel ill or incapacitated with a body ache, an upset stomach, or even a heavy dose of the blues, this ally reaches into the healing pouch and hands me the perfect remedy. Guess what? You too are fortunate to have a friend like mine who can prescribe that saving ounce of prevention or provide a timely remedy for what ails you. You can call this friend your inner guide, inner healer, inner helper, health adviser, or whatever name you wish. I call this inner source of healing insights from my intuitive mind, my "inner physician."

Intuition is that unerring and inexplicable knowing beyond logic and volition. It lies at the roots of spontaneity, humor, creativity, inspiration, and even genius. And it is an especially powerful ally in the healing process. Intuition is also the mind of our inner physician.

The medical missionary, theologian, and music scholar Albert Schweitzer was speaking of the inner physician when he said, "The medicine man succeeds for the same reason all the rest of us succeed. Each patient carries his own doctor inside him. We are at our best when we give the doctor within each patient a chance to go to work." As the inner physician, your intuitive mind is on constant alert to warn you of impending health challenges, present remedies to eradicate debilitating stress, reverse conditions of ill health, and help you develop improved habits for maintaining optimal health.

One of the ways my inner physician alerts me to a potential crisis is through my dreams. Let me share an example. I dreamed that a doctor gave me a diagnosis of cancer. In my dream I was astounded by the pronouncement, and I called the doctor a quack for trying to make me believe I had this dreadful disease. Months after the dream, I made an appointment with a skin doctor to have a red bump on my nose examined. As I lay on the table, I felt a surge of pain in my nose from a deep incision. I looked up to see the doctor sewing up my nose. I was appalled! After all, I had just come for an *opinion* about the bump. The doctor explained that he needed to cut a piece out of my nose for a biopsy to ascertain if I had skin cancer. He was already convinced I did and urged me to prepare myself for a series of cancer treatments.

My head was spinning. Then I recalled my dream and realized his statement mirrored the dream scenario, suggesting to me that this doctor was wrong. As it turned out, the bump was benign, yet the doctor insisted I have the series of cancer treatments anyway. Guided by my inner physician, I refused the treatments despite the doctor's recommendations. Weeks later, a second doctor gave me a clean bill of health. This dream alert from my intuitive mind foreshadowed the first doctor's erroneous diagnosis and prepared me to act wisely. And it brought home an important lesson: no matter what any "outer" doctor says, get a second opinion from your inner physician.

The Promise

You hold a book in your hands that promises to connect you with your inner physician. Why are you reading this book? Are you ill and seeking recovery? Are you well and seeking a way to maintain optimum health? Are you looking to discover the secrets of inner healing? By accessing your inner physician, you will accomplish all of the above.

Over a hundred years ago Thomas Edison said, "The doctor of the future will give no medicine but will interest his patients in the care of the human frame, in diet, and in the cause and prevention of disease." You are putting Edison's words into action by reading this book—a book filled with insights and steps to help you achieve and maintain good health, the most precious commodity in the world.

Could Edison walk down the corridors of history to the present, he would be delighted but not surprised to see our growing awareness of the powerful body/mind connection. Countless magazine and newspaper articles and attendance at cutting-edge seminars provide evidence that body/mind therapies are being widely utilized by an increasing number of practitioners and ordinary people. Consequently, traditional medical and more holistic practices are becoming more intertwined. Through the celebrated writings of many holistic practitioners, such as Drs. Joan Borysenko, Larry Dossey, Bernie Siegel, Andrew Weil, and others, we realize that we are no longer simply at the mercy of bacteria and viruses. Now we have access to a weapon stronger than any disease, the power of the mind, which can combat and even turn around the course of many degenerating illnesses. Dr. Caroline Myss elegantly reminds us of the energy medicine credo, which states: "I am responsible for the creation of my health. I therefore participated, at some level, in the creation of this illness. I can participate in the healing of this illness by healing myself, which means simultaneously healing my emotional, psychological, physical, and spiritual being."

Tipping the Scales

Goethe said, "Coming events cast their shadows beforehand." The same is true of illness. Signs are almost always given. Yet many of us are immobilized when the alarm sounds. Our inner physician or intuitive mind can alert us to an emergency or impending disaster by sending precognitive warnings in the form of images, dreams, and gut feelings, preparing us for appropriate action when the time comes. And it also sends us advance warnings when we are facing illness or disease. But we must learn to look for and recognize these signs, taking appropriate action to recover our balance and restore or maintain our health.

Through this book you will learn effective ways of connecting with the intuitive mind and receiving invaluable information and insights. A powerful technique for accomplishing this is the Mindshift Method, which is a bridge or doorway from your logical mind to that mysterious intuitive realm within you containing a vast storehouse of healing wisdom.

This book will help you tip the scales in the direction of optimal health. You will find anecdotes, words of wisdom from the experts, and exercises and techniques to inspire you to work on your health from the inside. You will learn to access your intuitive self, or inner physician, who communicates in many ways—by means of hunches or flashes of insight or knowledge; in daydreams, fantasies, or mental pictures; and through dreams rich in symbolism and imagery.

Nancy, a woman in midlife, had her uterus and ovaries removed after doctors spotted a cancerous growth in that area. Still alert to any recurrence, the doctors kept Nancy under strict observation, an anxiety-provoking situation for anyone. Nancy managed to calm herself after her inner physician came to her in a dream in which she received a gift certificate for a tank of gas. In her dream, she drove over a hill, and at the bottom on the other side, noticed her gas tank was empty. She filled the tank up in the nick of time. The meaning was obvious and reassuring to her. She literally felt like she was over the hill with her health crisis and was once again going through life with a full tank.

One theme of this book is that you can enjoy radiant good health. However, though miraculous healings do occur, it is simplistic to assume that you can read this book, apply a Mindshift Method practice, and instantly turn a devastating illness into well-being. What you can get, though, is a breakthrough perspective by means of which you can see the deeper meaning of any ailment, know what steps to take to address its causes, and begin the process of healing. Along the way you may have to change your physical regimen and old, unhealthy patterns of thought, emotion, and belief.

This book is a map of the Wellness Trail, a path to walk for a lifetime, guided by your inner physician. It will also show you how you can reach out to help others in need of healing. Your inner physician is intuitively aware of the condition of those you love, family and friends who may need your help, and often provides you with health alerts for them.

For example, a student of mine who worked in the automotive industry was concerned about his friend's health. While he was using the Mindshift Method for his friend, his intuition sent him the image of a broken radiator with steam coming out at different points. He realized his friend had a serious health problem. When he shared this hunch, his friend was utterly skeptical. At my student's insistence, the friend finally scheduled a doctor's appointment and found out that he indeed had a serious heart problem. Tests revealed a life-threatening blockage, but this early attention prevented a major heart attack.

Access to your inner physician increases your response-ability in maintaining every facet of well-being. You will learn how to eradicate the thoughts, language patterns, beliefs, and actions that have limited your ability to stay healthy and happy in the past. With the guidance of your inner physician, you will create a new life-affirming context for your life and the lives of those around you.

The Book's Intuitive Path

Through this book you will be initiated step by step into ways to reach and use the wisdom and healing powers of your inner physician. As you will discover, your body/mind is an intuitive antenna constantly transmitting and receiving messages from within and without. You will learn to decipher the messages of your intuitive mind and even of your dreams, which are a natural source of healing wisdom. The Mindshift Method will allow you to move beyond the barrier of your logical mind into the presence of your inner physician. Using this process you will be able to enter a deeply relaxed, intuitive state, define a problem or issue, and ask for and receive diagnoses, remedies, and healing insights into a variety of health conditions. You will learn to become centered and to release the physical, mental, and emotional tensions that contribute to nearly all illness.

You will also learn to use imagery to communicate with your body/mind and your inner physician; and to shift from despair or negativity to a positive, healing perspective that will have a direct impact on your state of mind and body. You will read several case studies showing how others have used the Mindshift Method to find resolutions to baffling, seemingly insoluble health problems.

You will learn to do a body scan, to enter into any area of distress and discover which body/mind connections need to be realigned. You will learn to elicit imagery that will reveal how stress is manifesting itself in your body. And finally, you will learn how to align the physical, mental, emotional, and spiritual facets of your being and reach the inner power or presence at your center that can dissolve all stress and bring healing peace.

The last chapter contains a brief review and final exercise that will help you assess your current life and health goals and find the motivation to take the steps recommended to you by your own inner physician.

Now it is time to start walking the Wellness Trail in Chapter 1. Before you begin, remember that you already have the power to think yourself well and to call on the tremendous healing resources within you when confronting any major health challenge. Positive thoughts, acts, beliefs, and emotions are the spiritual food that create a happy, healthy body. Even now your inner physician is waiting to guide you into the state of radiant health that you desire and deserve.

The

INTUITIVE

HEALER

Chapter One

THE INTUITIVE VOICE SPEAKS

T he following story demonstrates the wonderful workings of the intuitive mind. Judge Thomas Brennan, president of the Thomas Cooley Law School, wasn't feeling up to par. He had seen several doctors, but each one had told him, "There's nothing wrong with you." Finally he went to the Mayo Clinic. The doctor there gave him test after test; he just didn't like something about the judge's thyroid. Although there was no clear-cut problem, the doctor continued to search for the source of the something. After days of testing, the doctor tried a rarely administered blood test called a Talactin test and discovered that the judge had a Talactin count of 1,800 (the normal count is 25 or 30), caused, the doctor discovered, by a nonmalignant pituitary tumor that could be controlled with medication. The doctor's decision to follow his intuition, to keep probing until he found the real culprit behind the judge's malaise, helped him succeed where all the other experts had failed. This is the mark of a true healer—an *outer* physician connected with the judge's *inner* physician.

This chapter will show you how you too can receive guidance from your inner physician. The first step is to identify how your intuitive voice communicates with you.

THE MANY VOICES OF INTUITION

Your intuitive mind has many kinds of voices. Some people hear an actual voice telling them how to proceed. Others may see, feel, taste, or smell the messages relayed by the intuitive mind. Your intuition may communicate through words, symbols, energy, simple awareness, or inner wisdom. Here are some samplings of intuitive messages:

> I *heard* a little voice tell me to get a second opinion.
> I *see* myself engaging in more exercise.
> I know this is the right prescription—it just *feels* right.
> I have a good *taste* in my mouth about the new chiropractor.
> I don't want these new supplements. They don't *smell* right to me.

Your inner physician, also known as your intuition, can speak in a whisper or a shout to get your attention. Your intuition communicates through all your senses. One of my graduate students, a nurse, was examining a patient who had come in for a routine appendectomy. To her surprise she heard an inner voice repeating the word *colon*. When they opened the patient up, it turned out that he did indeed have perforations of the colon that required surgery. This confirmed the diagnosis of the nurse's inner physician. In addition to *hearing* the correct diagnosis, she might have received intuitive messages through any of her other senses. Suppose she *saw* a calendar in her mind's eye with the next seven months bordered in red. This would suggest a recuperation time longer than that of a routine appendectomy. In her initial examination of the patient, she might have imagined a foul *smell* coming from his stomach or had the sensation of a sour *taste* in her mouth, also indicating a more serious health ailment. Or the *touch* of the patient's hospital record might have reminded her of sandpaper, suggesting a rough time ahead.

Can you identify the voice of your intuition? Is it an inner voice telling you to "Get a second opinion"? Or is it more like a flash out of the blue urging you to change your diet by cutting out red meat? Maybe your intuition speaks in mental pictures floating in front of you, flashing images that contain important messages. Have you ever felt a persistent, even nagging *sense* about a person or situation? All these are the voices of your intuition.

PRACTICE: IDENTIFY YOUR INTUITIVE VOICE

I often say to my husband, "Can you *hear* what I'm saying?" He usually responds, "I *see* what you mean." My characteristic language is auditory and his is visual. Identify how you perceive the intuitive voice by noticing how you bring any of the five senses into your ordinary conversation. Here are some other examples. "I can *smell* trouble a mile away." "I can *see* the tension in your body." "I can *hear* my mother saying, 'Don't forget to take your vitamins.' " As you become more aware of your language, write down the sentences you say in life that reveal which senses you use. _____

_____
_____
_____
_____

Which sensory modality is dominant? _____

_____
_____
_____

MEETING YOUR INNER PHYSICIAN

Discovering your intuition opens the door to your inner physician, who is at your service to help you create and maintain optimal health. Other possible terms for the inner physician or intuitive mind include "higher self," "higher consciousness," "creative mind," "essence," or "godlike energy." I will use the terms "intuitive mind" and "inner physician" interchangeably within this book.

When I trust my inner physician, I am amazed at the wise insights and the stream of clever communication I receive. Remarkably, you can gain information from your inner physician that will complement the data provided by the latest advances in medicine and science. Remember the story about a former student of mine who was intuitively alerted to a friend's health crisis? The friend resisted, but eventually he went to the doctor, and my student had been right all along: trouble was brewing in his friend's body.

PRACTICE: MEET YOUR INNER PHYSICIAN

Find a place where you will not be disturbed for at least ten minutes. Sit in a comfortable chair or lie on a bed or on the floor. Make sure your back is straight and your hands and feet are uncrossed. Close your eyes. Take several slow, deep breaths. In your imagination, travel to a favorite locale, a place you know and have visited, or a retreat you have created in your mind. (I always go to a particular stretch of beach on Paradise Island in the Bahamas.) Once you are there, ask to meet your inner physician. Then notice what impression presents itself to you. Don't try to make anything happen. Just sense what bubbles up in response to your question. Is it an image of someone you know or someone you don't? Is it an image of a fictitious person or even an animal? Perhaps you sense an abstract form or color or energy, or see a symbol like the medical caduceus or a lotus flower. You may not see anyone or anything but simply have a sense that you are connecting with your inner physician. Once you have made the initial contact, you don't have to do anything more. Before opening your eyes, agree how and where you can meet again. Record the details of your experience.

Meeting place: _____

_____

_____

My inner physician: _____

_____

_____

Next meeting: _____

_____

_____

Defining Intuition

What is intuition? I define it as a clear knowing without being able to explain how one knows, or as knowledge gained without logical or rational thought. Intuition is the receipt of information from a nonphysical database. On a grander scale, intuition makes available the unlimited knowledge and wisdom that resides within, the deepest wisdom of the human soul. The title of a book by Marlo Morgan perfectly describes intuition: *The Mutant Message Down Under.*

Using an image as a metaphor, intuition is like a lightning flash of knowing that strikes from another dimension. It opens the door to further understanding and resolves indecision. Intuition can also be conceived as a satellite dish that picks up signals in the form of images, ideas, and feelings and beams them onto the screen of your conscious awareness.

PRACTICE: DEFINING INTUITION

How do you define intuition? Let your logical mind provide the words and your intuitive mind give you the pictures.

The words are _____

_____

_____

The picture is _____

_____

_____

Many people feel they are not intuitive because they don't use the word "intuition." Here are some of the words that I have heard others use to describe intuition: "hunch," "inspiration," "gut feeling," "vision," "Aha!" "educated guess," "judgment call," "sixth sense," "ESP," "insight," "business acumen," "premonition, "shooting from the hip," or even "flying by the seat of your pants." One reason people assign less value to intuition than they should is that they associate it with sloppy or irrational thinking. Or it becomes known as a woman's thing, not available to men. But if intuition were a skill possessed only by women, men would be cut off from one of the greatest sources of creativity and wisdom.

More and more people are becoming aware that the rich inner

resource of intuition is available to everyone. In business, for example, successful leaders have learned to rely on power hunches (i.e., intuition) to help them achieve personal and professional success. Artists, educators, politicians, and people in every walk of life are now actively cultivating this universal gift.

You can build a relationship with your intuitive mind almost anywhere: in the office, on a commuter train, walking, relaxing, even sleeping. Intuition—your inner adviser, inner instructor, inner consultant, inner colleague, or inner counselor—can speak to you at any point, day or night. This internal dialogue was second nature for Dr. Jonas Salk, the discoverer of the polio vaccine; for Thomas Edison, prolific inventor; for Carl Jung, brilliant psychologist; for Jeane Dixon, gifted clairvoyant; and many more. "Others may not be conscious that they conduct this type of dialogue," said Jonas Salk, "but they do. Why should it only happen to me?"

The more you work with your intuition, the more it can help you in every part of your life: making decisions in your professional life and in relationships; sparking your creative flow; helping you communicate clearly with others; understanding yourself and your body better; and making proactive decisions to maintain optimal health.

My friend and colleague Dr. Jeffrey Mishlove, president of the Intuition Network, provides a perspective on the workings of the intuitive mind. He feels that as we go beyond the realm of competitiveness with one another, we inevitably question some of our deepest values. When we look at the bigger picture of our life, we intuitively probe to find out "What is good?" "What is beautiful?" "What is sacred?" "What is balanced?" and "What is just?" Each of us has the potential to create a world where practicality and sacredness are one. Jeffrey elegantly states that "through intuition, we apprehend our fundamental interconnectedness with and love for all beings."[1]

Intuition Is Only Part of the Story

Let me assert at the outset that I am a whole brain advocate. I never promote strict adherence to intuition alone. That would be like a bird or plane flying on one wing. Intuition and logic together constitute a dynamic duo within you, waiting to guide you through your daily activities and spur you to make your dreams come true. We must integrate intuition with logic in order to function effectively, to become whole and complete.

While I recognize that becoming a whole person requires both intuition and logic, this book emphasizes the faculty of intuition—which I lovingly call the sleeping giant within—because it is usually underutilized and rarely acknowledged in our everyday affairs. Once intuition is aroused, this remarkable resource can be tapped regularly and reliably. Exercising your intuitive muscle will become a routine part of your everyday activities. The more you use this muscle, the more available your inner physician becomes. Keeping a diary and working with dreams are two ways of building intuitive muscles.

The Dream Alert

Sometimes the intuitive directive comes like that proverbial flash out of the blue or through a dreamlike reverie. My own intuitive doorway opened through a dramatic dream: I was driving a car, and when I put my foot on the brake it went right to the floor. The car turned over and I got out unharmed. Weeks later I was coming from a dance rehearsal, driving down a heavily trafficked street in Washington, D.C., when I put my foot on the brake and it went right to the floor, just as in the dream. The emergency brake didn't work, either. At just that moment I heard a voice say, "Make a quick right," and I crashed between two clothing stores, the only area of safety.

Dreams can be a very important source of intuitive guidance. They often provide a preview of upcoming events and advise you as to what step to take next. Often I don't hear my intuitive voice during the day, but rather in the still of the night, when I am receptive. Then my intuitive voice may speak through a dream to provide direction, guidance, or a warning. A dream can put me in direct touch with my subconscious, the source of intuitive wisdom and home of my inner physician.

The relationship of dreams and the intuitive mind has always fascinated me. I'll never forget a story I heard at a dream conference in Virginia Beach. A woman with stomach cancer had exhausted all the traditional remedies. One night during a dream, she was visited by a long-deceased uncle who came to give her a healing remedy for her cancer. He simply said, "Eat a can of hearts of palm for the next thirty days." The woman was amused and bewildered, as she had never even heard of hearts of palm. However, she followed her dead uncle's advice and astounded everyone thirty days later, when her cancerous condition slipped into remission.

The Subconscious Realm

If you don't yet recognize your intuitive voice, let me assure you that by reading these pages and completing the exercises in this book, you will learn how to recognize, develop, and reach your intuition. As you go inside yourself to retrieve incredible advice from your inner physician, you will notice how those insights lead to a remarkable improvement in your physical health and overall well-being. By doing this, you are drawing on a huge reservoir of wisdom within you in an area that some psychologists call the subconscious. You may have heard the term "subconscious" used in another context. I like to compare this subconscious to a giant computer database that contains all the information you can possibly need, including memories, creative ideas, wisdom, and knowledge. Any time you need a new insight or perspective about your health, you can retrieve it from this fount of universal knowledge, in a flash of awareness or insight from your subconscious. Whereas the conscious mind is regimented—it tends to come in the front door—the subconscious mind is not inhibited; it will come via the back door, through the windows, or even down the chimney. Even though intuition resides in the subconscious, its reach extends far beyond the subconscious into mysterious realms.

The internal environment of the subconscious is vibrant. To enter this exciting realm, you first need to silence the mental noise and relax your body in order to become more receptive to the input from all your senses. Dr. Jonas Salk said, "The intuitive mind will tell the thinking mind where to look next." You become aware of the constant interaction of conscious and subconscious minds as your hunches and insights direct your actions in the outer world.

Your intuition operates to uncover the truth and wisdom from this world within you. When I teach, lecture, or talk to clients and allow myself to be spontaneous, I surprise myself with the pearls of wisdom that roll out of my mouth. For example, I told a friend to be careful not to overexercise. The next day, he called to tell me he had torn a cartilage when he extended the number of miles he was jogging!

You will feel an incredible excitement when you connect with your intuitive mind. I first became aware of the power of my intuitive mind twenty-five years ago. I am still amazed at how I am led to contact people I have never met, come upon creative solutions my rational mind can't begin to imagine, and find ingenious ways to present my material to the world. When I first became aware of my intuitive mind, I noticed that when I was counseling my clients I would say something downright brilliant and would wonder how I retrieved that information. I later came to realize that the information came *through* me, not *from* me. In subsequent years, my intuition has served me superbly, guiding me through dangerous or unfamiliar situations and helping me translate or verbalize this process to people unfamiliar with the workings of the intuitive mind. The books I have written have all come through me as well. They have never been laborious, but rather have been acts of love.

PRACTICE: SPOT YOUR SERENDIPITOUS
OR SPONTANEOUS INSIGHTS

Whether or not you know it, you have always benefited from the workings of your intuitive mind. I can show this to you through this spontaneity check. I want you to clear your mind of all thoughts of work, responsibility, or things you feel you must do. Find a quiet spot and get comfortable in your chair—or if you prefer, lie down on the floor. Take three deep breaths. Imagine that you are looking at a circle that turns into a rose. Focus momentarily on this flower. If you have difficulty visualizing, simply relax your body, let it open like a flower, in a receptive mode, and feel the pulse of your being. Now ask your intuitive mind to help you recall those memories or times when you said or did something uncharacteristic that brought comfort or relief to another person or introduced an innovative concept at work. For example, have you made suggestions at work and later wondered where those ideas came from? Did you give sage advice to a friend that just hit the spot? Become aware of the workings of your intuitive mind by listing these recollections. _____

_____

_____

_____

_____

Read on to find out how the intuitive mind can unlock the secrets of radiant health.

KEYS TO RADIANT HEALTH

Ten intuitive keys will open the doorway to radiant health and connect you with your inner physician. The first version of these keys was presented in my book *Dr. Marcia Emery's Intuition Workbook*.

Key 1. *Your body is an intuitive antenna.* You will encounter a wealth of relevant information as you become increasingly attuned to the messages your body provides. Those stomach pains may not be the sudden onset of the flu. Instead of reaching for the aspirin, examine what you can't stomach about a situation. For example, if the pains started after an unpleasant encounter with your secretary, who is reluctant to assume more responsibility for office detail, your gut may have been signaling you that you couldn't *stomach* her limp excuses.

Key 2. *Honor your flashes and hunches.* Don't regard any as silly, weird, or coincidental. That gut feeling or inner message coming from you to you is about that most precious commodity, your health. One way to honor these hunches and flashes is to record them in a journal or idea book. No longer will you say, "I should have listened to my gut." Now you are being goaded into action.

Key 3. *Express your hunches concisely, using only a word or two.* The intuitive mind is simple and responds pointedly without lengthy discourse. Suppose you asked me "How do you feel?" The reply flashing immediately from my intuitive mind is "Like sunshine." If I gave you a paragraph or two about all my joys or pains, I would be responding from my logical mind, which is verbal and provides details. When you become wordy, you have moved out of your intuitive mind. At the beginning of my seminars, I ask people to close their eyes, to become centered and quiet. I ask them to let two words come up to describe what they are feeling at that moment. They share words such as "excited," "anticipatory," "rushed," "eager," and "expectant." When someone starts to wax eloquent, I give a gentle reminder to come back to the intuitive mind.

Key 4. *The intuitive mind speaks in pictures, symbols, and images.* The image you get from my "like sunshine" example is very vivid. You can sense that I am feeling bright and optimistic today.

In contrast, a man feeling depressed might talk about being under a dark cloud. Do you get the picture? That is what the intuitive mind is all about—sending you the picture. Suppose you asked the question "Should I have a heart transplant?" and spontaneously received a picture or symbol of garden tools. What would this say to you? You will find out how to interpret this puzzling symbolism in the next key.

Key 5. *Freely associate to the imagery you receive.* This will help you unravel the underlying meaning of any symbol. Keep making associations to the image until the "Aha!" comes forth. Let's go back to our example of the possible heart transplant in Key 4. At my suggestion that you begin associating to the garden tools, you come up with words like "spring flowers," "retool," "useful," "basic earth," "prepare the soil," "plant seeds," "weed," and "hoe." When you say "spade," your eyes light up, indicating that this is a key word. Further associations to the spade image lead you to think of "turn over" and then to "fresh start." This would tell you that a heart transplant will bring forth new life.

I also consulted with another person who wanted to know if he should adopt a new health supplement. After shifting to the intuitive mind, he saw a turtle. The associations were "slow," "green," "animal," and "hard shell." When the "Aha!" of "stick your neck out" came, he felt that this intuitive solution was correct. As you make your own associations, you will discover the punny nature of the intuitive mind. You might see a friend as a *bear* and then realize that he or she speaks the *bare truth* or is willing to *bare* himself or herself before others.

Key 6. *Pay attention to first impressions.* If you had a dime for every time in the past ten years you said, "I should have gone with my first impression," you would have enough money to treat yourself to a first-class Hawaiian vacation. Whenever I talk to a group about the keys, someone *always* comes up afterward to reinforce my message about first impressions. This has been especially poignant when people smelled a lemon when buying a product but went ahead with the purchase, only to discover later that their hunch or first impression of "don't buy" was correct.

Many people accurately press the first-impression button when receiving a diagnosis that just doesn't feel right. This usually means that your inner physician is at work, steering you to get a second opinion.

Key 7. *Attend to the faint stirrings as well as the loud raps.* The intuitive mind speaks subtly and nudges you gently. Only in extreme cases when you don't pay attention will you be hit over the head by a cosmic two-by-four as a wake-up call. This is what I meant earlier when I said, "Your inner physician, also known as your intuition, can speak in a whisper or a shout to get your attention." When your inner physician tugs at your sleeve, offering a second opinion, notice it. Is it a murmur in your ear or a jerk at your sleeve?

Key 8. *Become alert to passive signals, like flashes, or actively probe for an intuitive reply.* Sometimes our intuitions flash rapidly into our minds. We can be out jogging, walking the dog, or sitting at a desk when an insight or the answer to a dilemma bursts in the door unannounced. I prepare for these serendipitous insights by carrying a little notebook and pen. You too can be ready for these intuitions that come spontaneously. Another way to access intuitive information is to actively ask a question and probe for the reply. Have you ever agonized over a yes-or-no decision, even asking other people for their opinions? There are many ways you can create imagery to signal a yes-or-no reply. I like to visualize a traffic light in my mind. The green light is the go-ahead signal, the red tells me to put on the brakes, and the yellow encourages me to proceed cautiously.

Key 9. *Relaxation enhances receptivity.* When people tell me they have difficulty engaging in brainstorming activities, I know they are stuck in their logical mind. The pathway to more creative and innovative responses is blocked when the problem-solving mind travels well-worn routes. Switching the route over to the intuitive mind introduces the problem to a new realm filled with unconsidered options. Relaxation is needed so you become more receptive as you switch from the logical mind to the inspired intuitive mind. Working from a home office, I tend to labor long hours. I rarely escape to the beach or a more palatable setting. The ringing phone, overflowing mail bins, and stacks of to-do folders constantly remind me of work. When my husband and I need a getaway, we go to the nearest motel for rest and repair. I always promise myself and Jim that I will relax and not do any "work." The scene is always the same. Minutes after I am submerged in the motel's Jacuzzi, I jump up, get a pad, and start writing ferociously. Jim always questions whether I am living up to my vow not to work. For me, the answer is simple. When I relax, all these wonderful new ideas come floating into my head because I am completely receptive to my intuitive mind. The challenge is learning how to relax anywhere without waiting to be transported to such a setting.

Key 10.   *Have fun and be playful courting your intuitive self.* The resilient and playful intuitive mind loves to have fun. It is like a young child gleefully jumping up and down at the playground. Let your intuitive punster or prankster bring mirth and hilarity into the situation. Levity opens the intuitive mind. I always have some of my favorite cartoons handy to give me a laugh and help me stoke the creative fire. Right now, I am glancing at one of my favorite cartoons, which shows a man holding large cymbals in his hand and looking at a musical score; the music is entitled "Man and His Cymbals, by Carl Jung." This always amuses me, since one of my favorite books is Carl Jung's *Man and His Symbols*. My favorite cartoon strips always give me a chuckle. I even dip into the memories of truly funny moments I've shared with my mom or husband. If you haven't started a cartoon collection, this is a wonderful time to do so. Read the funnies or buy a joke book. Not only will you agree that laughter is the best medicine, but you'll discover another side benefit as you fling open the spacious corridors of your intuitive mind.

PRACTICE: KEY INTO INTUITION

Try exercising your intuitive muscle with some of the keys. Here is how you can practice using Key 4. As you become more adept at contacting your intuitive mind, you can prepare for a meeting or a discussion with someone by asking to see a picture of how the encounter will proceed. Record here the way you envision a future meeting or discussion proceeding. Note as many details as possible. For example, what does the room look like? Where are people sitting in relation to one another? How do people seem to be relating to one another? Do people appear happy, relaxed, irritated, or nervous? Can you visualize a successful outcome of the meeting? What would that look like? _____

_____

_____

Here is how you can actively probe for an intuitive reply using Key 8. Take a moment now to pose any question to your intuitive mind that requires a yes-or-no answer. You might pose a weighty question such as, "Should I change my doctor?" or something more routine: "Should I take a double dose of vitamin C?" Take a few deep breaths to shift to the intuitive mind. To become more centered, imagine that you are looking at a triangle. Hold that image for three seconds and then elicit a traffic signal with three lights. Pose your question and notice which light comes on. Does the green give you the yes, or go-ahead, signal? Does the red light tell you to stop or say no? Or does the yellow light say "Proceed cautiously"? ____

_____

_____

Become aware of Key 7's faint stirrings by recalling the times you had a hunch to go to the doctor or a gut feeling to check out a new treatment or vitamin. Did you heed the gentle reminder? Did you need a strong prod to take action? Record your experience here. For example, can you remember the time you needed to take a break from working too hard and you didn't listen? Days after this internal warning nudged you to take a break, which you ignored, you came down with the flu. _____

_____

_____

PARADIGM SHIFTS: BUILDING A
NEW MOUSETRAP

Another key ingredient for accessing your inner physician is shifting your paradigm. Here's how it works. Have you ever been presented with an idea or proposal to which you replied, "It can't be done"? I think we all forget from time to time that our mind is like a parachute: it functions only when it is open. Yet we *can* reinvent the wheel and discover a hula hoop or a better mousetrap. We just need to believe that it *can* be done. We need to replace our old ideas or models with new paradigms that open us to greater possibilities.

Can you recall a time in your life when you stood up to all the naysayers in your environment who said something couldn't be done? Many years ago, my determination to write a book about intuition and show people in the business arena how to cultivate this skill was met with snickers. Yet through my earlier book, *Dr. Marcia Emery's Intuition Workbook: An Expert's Guide to Unlocking the Wisdom of Your Subconscious Mind*, many people found out that teaching people how to cultivate their intuition could be done. When I need a nudge to move out of the "I can't" corner into the arena of knowing that it can be done, I recall Albert Einstein's wonderful words: "No problem is solved by the same consciousness that created it." When the logical mind says it can't be done, a shift to the intuitive mind shows how in fact it can!

Making the Shift

Have you ever acted in a way that was so atypical that you had people wondering if you were in your right mind? This happened to me quite recently when I had an excruciating toothache. Most people simply call and make an appointment to see their dentist, but I had just moved across the country and had no dentist as yet. I wasn't quite ready to trust my precious mouth to a stranger.

When I consulted my inner physician, the reply I got was "Wait, relief will come." Then I heard, "You will be shown the way in a most unorthodox manner." I simply opened up to the wisdom of my intuitive mind, knowing I would be led appropriately. It's hard to forget a toothache, but I temporarily put the question of what to do aside. Later, I was telling a new friend about the pain in my mouth and she immediately replied, "You need to see my Qi Gong doctor." I asked if he was a dentist. She said, "No, but he uses Qi Gong to restore balance in the energy field and bring relief." I had a strong hunch that I was being led to the right person. When I met Dr. Bingkun Hu, a Chinese acupressurist specializing in the ancient Chinese practice of Qi Gong, which guides the flow of Qi, or vital essence, for health and longevity, he taught me a series of movements. I enjoyed doing these because they triggered memories of my days as a dancer. However, I wasn't quite sure how these exercises would help alleviate the pain.

Days later I found out that these movements were creating the energy to help my mouth heal. During the second part of the session, I lay down on the massage table as the doctor alternated between gently manipulating the energy around my body and lightly patting certain bodily parts. When the hour was over, I felt like I was walking on a cloud. Amazingly, my pain was gone without any traditional dental treatment at all. By opening my mind to a new paradigm—a new way of treating this situation—my inner physician led me to a method that provided dramatic relief. My logical mind alone would never have entertained such a solution. But in tandem with the intuitive mind, the rational mind was able to suspend judgment and listen to the injunction "Trust me—wait and see."

PRACTICE: DISCOVERING YOUR HEALING BALM

The mysterious properties of chicken soup as a universal healer are legendary. Whether it's comfort food, a favorite vitamin, or some home remedy, we all use something as our personal "chicken soup" when we are indisposed. Have you ever changed your paradigm from a traditional remedy to something new?

If yes, what was your traditional remedy? _____

_____

_____

Was this something handed down through the family? _____

_____

What was the change you made? _____

_____

When you decided to make a change, how did the naysayers respond? _____

_____

Let your mind wander back to the first time you decided to try this method. How did the idea come to you? _____

_____

_____

Looking back, would you say you were intuitively inspired by the inner physician? _____

_____

_____

If you haven't had this experience, maybe you could try it now. What paradigm by way of any health practice would you like to change? _____

_____

_____

Ask your inner physician to send you a symbol or message of what first step you need to take. Then what steps do you need to do next? _____

_____

_____

Close your eyes and imagine you are incorporating this new paradigm. Describe how you feel and record what you are doing to bring this change about. _____

_____

_____

How comfortable are you with this new practice? _____

_____

_____

Now find a way you can anchor this paradigm shift in your daily life. How can you apply it and use it? For example, if you are trying to incorporate a new herbal remedy routine, you can put your herbs with your vitamins and write a daily schedule and put it on your mirror where you see it every day. Communicate your intentions to those close to you so they can help support you.

A SHIFT BY ANY OTHER NAME— THE MINDSHIFT

Shift does happen! With practice you will learn how to glide from the logical mind to the intuitive sphere with ease. Learning to shift consciousness from the logical or rational mind to the intuitive realm is the means of contacting your inner physician. This particular application of whole-brain thinking alleviates much of the stress created at work and through personal dilemmas, helping you cut quickly to the bottom line of a difficult problem to retrieve an innovative, creative, and viable approach. Let me remind you again that contacting your inner physician will help you optimize personal performance and attain radiant health.

The Mindshift Method you will be learning in this book guides beginners and experts alike through the crucial shift between the logical and intuitive minds. You'll learn how to (1) concentrate your mental energies, (2) increase your receptivity to mental imagery, (3) interpret those images, and most important, (4) implement the solutions provided by your intuitive mind. This formula, which I called Intuitive Problem Solving (IPS) in my first book, guides you every step of the way to breakthroughs in all aspects of your life, especially helping you see clearly the answers to life's thorniest health dilemmas. I first used the term Mindshift Method in the Nightingale Conant audiocassette album, *Intuition: How to Use Your Gut Instinct for Greater Personal Power*.

You have now had a taste of how the inner physician communicates with you, and you know you can receive a house call anytime of the day or night. In the next chapter, you will learn how to work with the dynamics of the Mindshift Method so you can readily traverse the terrain from your logical to your intuitive mind.

Chapter Two

INTUITION 911:
HOW TO CALL THE INNER
PHYSICIAN

You are only an hour away from surgery. You've read all the material about stomach cancer, collected all the facts, and received two medical opinions. Now you have to make a decision. Your doctor plans to operate, even though the second doctor's opinion is that an operation is unnecessary. You are aware of several alternative treatments, but you still don't know which direction to take. Although you respect the doctor who maintains that an operation is your only hope, his diagnosis doesn't *feel* right and your gut instinct is to go with the second opinion. After agonizing over the decision, going back and forth, you decide against the surgery. Later the next day, after receiving additional test results, you learn that your decision was well founded. Aren't you glad you followed your gut instinct?

A major operation is very risky. How can you be certain you are making the right decision? That is the essence of connecting with the intuitive mind. People all over the world rely on their gut instinct, or intuition, when they need to make life-or-death decisions. This inner ability is especially useful when you have to make a decision in a critical situation.

Your inner physician is always on call to respond to an Intuition 911 alert. The wisdom retrieved by making that call may be absolutely correct; the hitch is that you have to be certain that you are really accessing that pure fount of information. To ensure that your insights are not clouded, you need to eliminate any intruders masquerading as intuition and recognize the way in which these can stand in the way of true intuitive input.

The Intuitive Pretenders

There are a number of psychological and emotional conditions that can rob you of your intuitive voice. Wishful thinking, fear, ego, denial, fatigue, depression, projection, and stress can limit your ability to hear your inner physician. Learning to recognize these intuitive pretenders and then to minimize their power is necessary if you are to hear your intuitive voice. Let's take a look at some of these.

Wishful thinking obscures the real truth of a situation. Our wishes and hopes come from a fanciful space and tend to cloud our vision. This might happen after you have received a negative diagnosis and succumb to the Pollyannaish belief that this disease will never touch you. Dave, one of my therapy clients, had just lost his lover to AIDS. When his grief subsided, I asked Dave if he had taken an AIDS test. He was surprised at my question and emphatically said no. He then added, "I know God would not want such a thing to happen to me." His reply embodied a spiritual belief that he was invincible. Wishful thinking led him to believe he would be spared. Denial and fear may have kept him from taking the important step of being tested.

Fear often enters the scene after a dreaded disease has been diagnosed. When fear is racing through the mind, it becomes a challenge to hear the inner physician speak. For instance, an individual pushed into a fearful state after hearing a diagnosis of stomach cancer might not think it possible to transcend the disease. The power of the inner quadrangle of the body, mind, heart, and soul has the potential to heal almost any physical malaise. When fear reigns, however, these four musicians of your inner orchestra don't play together, making it impossible for you to hear your inner physician. Later in this chapter you will learn how to become centered and receptive when faced with any real or imagined health crisis, to quiet the fear and access your wise intuitive mind.

Getting the *ego* out of the way is important. Your ego can block the entrance to your inner physician's doorway. It is one of the major deterrents to intuitive awareness. When we assume the posture that we *know* how to do this or that, we are interfering with the knowledge coming from within. Pure intuition doesn't have any investment in the outcome and can see the larger picture. In contrast, when the ego stands in the way, a conscious or unconscious agenda is being followed. When you take the ego out of the situation, the intuitive spark is kindled.

When *projection* is at work, you are projecting your needs and wants onto someone else. Vehemently urging a friend to slow down might reflect a message that you are refusing to acknowledge from your own intuitive voice. By ignoring your inner physician's message to you, you remain on a collision course even as you steer your friend toward better health.

Stress can create highly negative emotional states that can so profoundly affect health that I've devoted Chapter 11 to explaining stress's multifaceted impact on our well-being. Corporations have invested untold amounts in their efforts to combat burnout and stress in the workplace. Stress management is imperative to help an organization's leaders and managers face corporate issues as whole people, not debilitated by pressure. People in burnout can't tell the difference between wishful thinking and intuition because their circuits are jammed. Contacting the inner physician is vital to developing proactive strategies to avoid burnout and debilitating stress.

Two additional offenders that dim the intuitive light cannot be overlooked: sabotaging yourself and downplaying your intuitive gift. Some people consciously or unconsciously sabotage success. Since intuition is the beacon that steers you onto the course to success, extinguishing that light prevents accomplishment. The success train is easily derailed when you don't trust that needed answers can come from within. Often, people are given intuitive information but discount this precious inside scoop.

Some people are very intuitive in the professional arena but don't trust the light of intuition at home. I have observed highly successful businesswomen who discount their intuitive muscle at home by deferring to a partner who, they have been taught, "knows best." In the home setting, they become people pleasers, acquiescing to the apparent insights of others while ignoring their own. And some people are cautious about acknowledging the validity of intuition because they are afraid they will not be taken seriously.

Working with the techniques in this book will help you surmount these and other obstacles so that you can access your intuition regularly and reliably. An aerospace engineer I knew admitted that he suppressed his intuition, because as a man of science, he believed that he needed to collect data and evidence for validation before trusting his inner voice.

This is a good time to notice what barriers impede your intuitive flow. Observe the ways you have been muffling your intuitive voice. Awareness is a significant step toward overcoming obstacles and climbing over the wall of self-imposed limitations into freedom, power, and radiant health.

PRACTICE: SURMOUNTING BARRIERS

What prevents you from listening to your hunches and gut feelings? Where does your resistance to relying on this silent but accurate partner come from? Do you try to examine every angle and amass all the facts before you act? Are you waiting for a doctor to give you one pill that will cure all? Do you feel that others know best? Do you fall into the trap of "This is not the way I've done it before"? Do you become immersed in negative, unproductive thoughts? Record the answers to these questions and examine your anti-intuitive strategies to gain insight into how your intuitive voice becomes stifled. _____

_____

_____

_____

_____

_____

_____

THE MINDSHIFT DANCE

The following technique will teach you to access your inner physician by shifting your awareness from the logical mind into the intuitive realm. Most of us spend considerable time eliciting input from our verbal logical mind. This is not surprising, since our culture overemphasizes the value of logic and verbal skills. The challenge comes when words and logic fail to resolve our dilemmas, to foretell the future, and to determine, for example, the validity of a diagnosis or recommended procedure, or even to reveal what crucial shift in attitude will put us onto the healing path. At this point, a shift to the intuitive mind is crucial.

Learning the Mindshift Method is very much like learning the steps to a new dance routine. The first few times you are aware of every step you repeatedly, laboriously perform. Soon, however, the steps become habitual and you enter into the rhythmic flow without a second thought. Here is a general overview of the Mindshift Method, which you will be using to access your intuitive mind.

- First you *define the problem or issue*.
- You become *centered* in order to release the mental tension.
- You release built-up physical tension and become more *receptive*.
- This helps you become more aware of the messages your intuition expresses through *imagery*, feelings, insights, and so on.
- Questions may arise as you continue to elicit and *interpret the symbols* generated by your intuitive mind.
- If the intuitive messages are still puzzling, step back to let the ideas seed and *incubate*.
- The intuitive response can stimulate other questions, which lead you to *further examine the responses*.
- Soon the "Aha!" will come forth so you can *implement a solution*.

Taking these steps to resolve elusive dilemmas is really simple, although the results are at times extraordinary. You are not shifting into any zombie-like dangerous state from which you will take months to recover. You are entering a natural state to discover what action is needed to restore you to optimal health.

As your inner physician comes forward, you will notice that your mind has become more still, your body has become more relaxed, your senses have become more open, and you can feel a current of subtle energy moving through and around you. This Mindshift Dance will eventually happen automatically and effortlessly. So let the dance begin as we take the first step together.

Step 1. *Define your issue.* Finding a successful resolution to your problem or concern is directly related to the clarity with which the issue is expressed. Often, what appears to be the major concern is actually background noise cloaking the *real* issue.

Much of your intuitive problem-solving will involve getting clarity. This applies to any problem, big or small. Perhaps you need to make an important decision about whether to commit to a particular health treatment. Perhaps you are trying to understand why your depressed mate can't reach out to people. You might want to know if a new physical regimen is right for you. You may seek a creative or innovative approach to managing a health concern, like taking herbs or changing your diet. Perhaps you want to resolve a personal issue, like switching to a healer or therapist who embraces a more holistic perspective.

As you formulate your issue, recall the third key to radiant health introduced in Chapter 1. Express your hunches in a word or two. Don't worry your problem—KISS it (keep it simple, sweetie!). The easiest way to get right to the bottom of an issue or problem is to couch it in the form of a question. Here are some examples: "When should I start my diet?" "Should I try Chinese herbs?" "How can I heal my weakened eye muscle?" "What type of treatment should I get for physical therapy?"

I always advise people not to formulate a double-barreled question. Here is an incorrect formulation: "How can I start a new physical exercise program *and* should I go on a diet?" These are two separate issues, each requiring a separate question. If I ask, "Should I go on a diet?" the answer will be yes or no. By asking "how," you are inviting a more graphic response. So be clear whether you want a simple yes or no or want to receive a variety of options about your inquiry.

Step 2. *Release mental tension and become centered.* What happens when you respond to the directive "Close your eyes and quiet your mind"? Can you do that readily? Whenever I teach people how to cultivate their intuition, I notice that very few people know how to quiet their mind. People who meditate daily can do this easily. You too will need to practice if you wish to cultivate this ability.

Start by taking a minute to become still. Acknowledge the thoughts that come into your mind by first observing them and then silently saying, "I'll get back to you later." For now, if finding stillness is difficult, know that you are not alone! Many people find that when they close their eyes, they walk into a noisy cocktail party in their mind. Through all that din, it is hard to hear the sound of the intuitive voice.

The logical mind is in the foreground when you frame and pose your question. As your centering activities begin, the intuitive mind comes forward and the logical mind retreats into the background. As you become centered by using one, some, or all of these suggested centering techniques, you will minimize the distracting inner chatter. These centering techniques include saying an affirmation, repeating a word, phrase, or prayer, focusing on a geometrical object or picture, and/or listening to slow music without vocals.

Say an Affirmation

Generate a positive statement that you will say a few times several times a day until you feel the effect of the words permeating your essence. You will know when the statement has penetrated into your consciousness. Can you imagine anyone walking around with a scowl after affirming, "I am the picture of radiant health"?

Let me start you off with a few health-related affirmations to inspire you until you create your own.

"My intuitive mind knows the right prescription for any health matter."

"My intuitive mind has infallible knowledge about healing my body."

"Every cell and organ of my body is being healed and renewed."

"The divine energy flowing through every cell of my body creates radiant health."

"My intuitive mind illumines me as healing energy courses throughout my body."

PRACTICE: CREATE A HEALTH AFFIRMATION

Create at least one affirmation you will say every day for the next two weeks. Record your experiences after doing this practice so you will notice that you are shifting into a positive perspective that embraces life with greater openness and clarity. _____

_____

_____

Two other techniques for becoming centered are repeating a focusing word or phrase and focusing on a geometrical object or picture.

Use a Verbal Focus or Mantra

Serenity! Serenity! Serenity! Try repeating this single word and experience its effect on your body/mind. Whenever you need to reconstitute your body, mind, heart, or soul, you can utter a comforting word or phrase. This is especially potent when you want to slow down the outer activity and hear what the inner mind has to say. By doing this, you are manipulating your brain waves to create a more relaxed state. These are ancient techniques used in every religion to achieve states of spiritual peace.

When I want to lower my brain-wave activity from its usual state at the beta level, which is measured at 13 to 25 cycles per second, I slow my breathing and use a focusing word. Then I slip into a more relaxed state of awareness at the alpha level, where the brain waves fall to 8 to 12 cycles per second. This state resembles that drifty feeling you experience when you awaken from a dream or a daydream. When your mind is in alpha, the intuitive mind truly comes out and will present you with innovative solutions and options that you never would have imagined with your logical mind functioning at beta. Your intuitive mind also flourishes at the theta level, when your brain waves lower to 5 to 7 cycles per second. You reach this level during sleep, hypnosis, or deep meditation. At the delta level, which occurs during deep or full sleep, your brain waves slow to 1 to 4 cycles per second.

You might prefer to use the word "mantra" instead of verbal focusing. You can select any meaningful word or use several words as your personal mantra. To become more intuitively receptive, I like to use focusing words such as "tranquillity," "calm," or "composure." I find phrases such as "peace be still" or "be still and know" quite effective for courting relaxation. When I ask my students about the phrases they have selected, I find out that some come from songs and others from literature and the Bible; some they composed by stringing together a few meaningful words.

PRACTICE: SELECT YOUR FOCUSING WORD AND PHRASE

Experiment by using several different focusing words that you think might help you become increasingly still. Do this with deep attention. By the process of elimination, determine which words feel most comfortable and suit you best. By invoking a focusing word, you will find yourself merging with that word. List the word or phrase that helps you become receptive. _____

_____

_____

What focusing word or phrase helps you feel centered? _____

_____

_____

Now repeat it with feeling randomly throughout the day, silently or aloud. Use it in moments of frustration, at work, in traffic. How do you feel? _____

_____

_____

How do you feel after saying this word or focusing phrase for two weeks? _____

_____

_____

Use a Visual Focus or a Mandala

Look around you right now. Find a geometrically shaped object and focus on it. (You can also use a candle flame.) Notice how the vociferous logical mind is quieted, allowing you to relax. Now notice any pictures, symbols, and metaphors that pop into consciousness from the intuitive mind. Geometric shapes known as mandalas have been used by various peoples all over the world. Their basic function is to help you become centered by quieting the talkative mind and shifting perception to an inner mode so the intuitive mind can create its own pictures. I use the terms "mandala" and "geometric picture" interchangeably.

I always hand out pictures of mandalas to my students and suggest they use them when they need to find equanimity in the work setting. I was delighted when one student, Craig, showed me that he kept one of these mandalas in his daily planner. When he needed to restore his equilibrium at work, he opened his planner and gazed at the mandala. This was especially effective during office meetings when dissension reigned.

By silencing the chatter coming from your logical mind, you will connect more readily with your inner physician. Then you will discover the mandalas in your environment, where symmetrical patterns are everywhere. You can find these natural geometric shapes on wallpaper, in carpets, in office plants, and everywhere in nature. You can also begin this centering process by focusing on objects around you such as plants, your wristwatch, or a ring on your finger. Some people prefer to look at a picture of a natural setting to help them relax. With practice, you will know which focusing object appeals most to you—a geometric design, a more natural mandala, an object, or a picture.

PRACTICE: DISCOVERING THE MANDALA

Focus on this geometric design for two minutes.

Record what you experience. _____
_____
_____
_____

Look around your office or home for mandalas such as wallpaper patterns, the wood grain of your desk, and the patterns in the rug. List all the mandalas you discover around you. _____
_____
_____
_____

Let's extend this to gazing at familiar objects. On my desk I have an amethyst with many purple facets and a special shell that was tossed up by the sea. I have a personal connection to both objects.

Either of them can serve as a focusing object. What focusing objects would you like to use? List at least one object that you feel a connection to and work with it. _____

_____

_____

Although you can connect with your intuition anytime and anywhere, notice how you gravitate to some areas in your surroundings; these are hot spots for intuitive receptivity. Just as spiritual traditions recommend meditating or praying in one place to empower it with spiritual vibrations, I suggest when you do your Mindshift practices, you designate an area in your home or office as your Mindshift Area. I made my office into a space where I get "hot flashes" all the time. Along with the amethyst and the shell, I have two incredibly scenic pictures on my wall of the blue-green surf hitting the rocks on Paradise Island in the Bahamas. Looking at these pictures transports me into the receptive alpha state. I also have two framed mandalas taken from a yearly calendar along with two cherished photos and quotes from my favorite mentor, Dr. Albert Einstein. I can gaze at any of these pictures to alter my awareness and be transported to the alpha level.

PRACTICE: GETTING THE PICTURE

Designate a space as your Mindshift area, where you will do your practices. _____

_____

What picture, object, or color will help you readily access your intuitive mind? _____

_____

_____

You can use all or select any of these four visual focusing techniques: the geometric mandala, the natural mandala, an object, or a picture of a natural scene. Try using each one for three days. Which is most effective to help you enter the receptive alpha state? _____

_____

_____

Step 3. *Release physical tension and become receptive.* Become still for a moment. Can you hear any noise in your head? If the cocktail party is still going on in your mind, return to centering techniques to quiet your mind. Once the mind has been quieted, it is time to eliminate or minimize any of your aches and pains and to calm the restless energies coursing through your body. Breathing and relaxation practices will help you release the physical tension and become more receptive.

In my classes and extended seminars, I present four breathing techniques and six relaxation practices. These are described in my book *Dr. Marcia Emery's Intuition Workbook: An Expert's Guide to Unlocking the Wisdom of Your Subconscious Mind.* Here are a breathing practice and a relaxation practice to jump-start your receptivity practice.

Breathing Techniques

When were you taught how to breathe? When you delivered a baby, took singing lessons, or attended a stress-reduction class? Most of us have never been taught how to breathe properly. If you take a moment or two to notice your breathing, it is probably very shallow. Now change that pattern. Sit erect, relax, and take a deep breath, counting to four as you inhale; hold the breath momentarily and then exhale as you count to four again. Can you feel the difference? Take five such breaths and notice what you feel. Is there a tingling in your head? Do your eyes see more clearly? Do you feel more alert? Does the room seem to shimmer slightly? For one week, take five minutes each morning before you begin your day to do one breathing practice. You will feel more energized, experience clarity, and most important, have immediate access to your intuitive mind.

Here is a breathing technique called the hang-sah breath. This breathing method, a yoga technique, has a dual function: it helps you slow your brain waves so you can enter the receptive alpha level, and it combats stress. Inhale and whisper "hang" as you lift the uvula in back of your throat just like when you are yawning. Then exhale and whisper "sah" like a sigh. You will rapidly feel relaxed when repeating this hang-sah breath several times.

―――――――――――――――――――――――――――――――――――――――
PRACTICE: EXPERIENCE THE HANG-SAH BREATH

Sit upright in a chair with your feet flat on the floor and your hands resting in your lap. Before beginning the hang-sah breath, affirm that you will avoid falling asleep by saying, "I will stay awake and become mentally alert while using the hang-sah breath." Repeat this affirmation three times.

Whisper aloud the word "hang" as you inhale and "sah" as you exhale. Continue inhaling as you whisper "hang" and exhaling as you whisper "sah" for ten more repetitions. Close your eyes and experience how you feel throughout your body. Open your eyes and record any observations of your experience from the hang-sah breath. _____

――

―――

Relaxation Techniques

I emphasized the importance of relaxation in the ninth key for opening your intuitive doorway in Chapter 1. Relaxation enhances receptivity. My intuitive mind is always engaged when I relax in a hot tub or Jacuzzi. There are many activities I find relaxing, but anything related to water seems to be effective for me and automatically stimulates my intuitive mind. Albert Einstein valued his periods of relaxation, which balanced the strenuous mental demands of his work. He loved to play his violin and relax on his sailboat. When I read that while he was in residence at Princeton University he liked to drift aimlessly in his canoe, I conjured up a wonderful image of Albert Einstein totally relaxed as the canoe slowly moved through the water. I have no doubt that during these times he became receptive to the profound discoveries that came through his intuitive mind.

With the tense-and-release technique, you imagine you are making a body area more tense in order to create a relaxed state. This practice helps you relax any tense or painful areas by tensing and releasing your muscles. If any spot stubbornly holds the tension, gently tell it to relax. As you practice, your body will listen more easily.

PRACTICE: EXPERIENCE THE "TENSE-AND-RELEASE" TECHNIQUE

Start by sitting in a comfortable chair or by lying on your back, arms and legs relaxed. Breathe in deeply through your nose and be aware of your chest rising and falling. Follow the current of air as it comes in through your nose. Be aware of the areas in your body that are being touched by this breath of life. Hold the air in and note how you feel. Finally, let the air come together from the various body parts to unite in a large current of air expelled from your nose or mouth. Imagine that you are exhaling all of the accumulated tensions of your being.

Use full, deep breaths for this practice.

- First inhale. Then curl your toes as tightly as you can while holding your breath.
- Exhale and relax your toes and feet. Repeat once more.
- Extend your legs straight out. Inhale, then tighten your leg muscles. Hold for a moment. Exhale and relax your legs. Repeat.
- Inhale again. Tighten your stomach and buttock muscles. Hold, then exhale and let these muscles relax. Repeat.
- Inhale. Make a fist with both hands and tighten the muscles in your arms. Hold for a moment, then exhale as you relax your arms. Repeat.
- Inhale. Tighten your shoulder and neck muscles. Hold, then exhale and relax your neck and shoulders. Repeat.
- Inhale. Tighten all the muscles in your face, clenching your teeth. Hold, then exhale as you let these muscles relax. Repeat.
- Take a deep breath, hold for a moment, and exhale.
- Close your eyes and be aware of how your body feels. Lie still for several minutes. Open your eyes and record your observations. What did you notice, feel, or experience during this practice? Which parts of your body feel relaxed? _____

_____

_____

_____

What areas still feel tense? _____

_____

_____

_____

For each of these areas, inhale, tighten the muscles, and imagine the area relaxing as you exhale.

Step 4. *Elicit imagery*. Eliciting imagery is vital for connecting with your inner physician as you call upon the intuitive help that lives within you. If you have difficulty eliciting imagery, you may want to revisit the practice activity in Chapter 1 where you identified your intuitive voice (see page 3). Look at the phrases you recorded and see what sensory words stand out. If you wrote "I *hear* you" and "I don't like the *look* of this," this indicates that your auditory and visual senses predominate.

Whenever the intuitive mind communicates by sending you pictures, symbols, or images, your imagination is working in high gear. The word "imagery" and "imagination" can be used interchangeably. In the last chapter, you were asked to retrieve memories. I challenge you to think of a memory in isolation without having a picture of image connected to it. It can't be done! Everyone has the capacity to elicit imagery.

Throughout their formal schooling years, most students are scolded for daydreaming and not paying attention. Daydreams have gotten a bad rap. They have become associated with fantasy and frivolity and are considered a waste of time by many. The Reverend Robert Schuller of the *Hour of Power* television ministry expresses this so well. He has said that nothing kills more dreams than two words: be realistic. Parents have a tendency to tell their kids to stop dreaming and get realistic. In reality, if people are encouraged to dream and formulate a vision, much greater accomplishments will result. Throughout your immersion in this book, you have my permission and encouragement to fantasize and daydream frequently so you can connect with the symbols, pictures, and images of your inner physician.

Continue to discover what senses you use to ignite the intuitive mind. In addition to the five senses of seeing, hearing, smelling, tasting, and touching, I am adding two auxiliary states. The affective sense reflects your inner emotions—feelings of joy, sadness, or anger. The kinesthetic sense, or your inner awareness of body movement, gives you the sense of flying, floating, or falling.

Here's another practice to ignite your senses. I'm going to ask you to mentally visit a favorite vacation spot where you will have the opportunity to connect with all your senses. Then you can identify which senses work strongly for you. My favorite locale is the beach, so I will take myself to our time-share in the Bahamas. Let me show you what I do to ignite all my senses. Some senses come in more strongly than others and thus need to be strengthened through practice.

My vacation fantasy starts by going to the airport and getting on the plane. Though the flight is smooth most of the way, I am aware of the occasional turbulence (kinesthetic). At the Nassau airport, I get off the plane and, upon entering the terminal, hear (auditory) the wonderful strains of the Bahamian merengue. I rent a car, and on the way to the hotel, I look out the window to ecstatically behold (visual) the beautiful palm trees blowing, the gorgeous blue-green water, and the wonderful sights along the narrow road as I wind my way to the hotel. My heart leaps with joy (affective). I see a stand where someone is selling conch salad and cracked conch. I park the car and relish tasting conch again (gustatory). When I see the beach across the road, I eagerly go over and take off my shoes and walk on the sand, which feels hot to my feet (tactile). Standing there, I can actually smell the seaweed from the ocean (olfactory). If I want more practice eliciting imagery, I can continue with this fantasy. The three strongest senses for me are the kinesthetic, the auditory, and the visual. My weakest sense is the olfactory. Now it is your turn to take yourself on your fantasy vacation. As the images and sensory perceptions arise in your consciousness, you will find out how your intuition speaks to you most clearly.

PRACTICE: CREATE A FANTASY TRIP

Prepare to take yourself to your favorite vacation spot. First get comfortable sitting in a chair, sitting on the floor, or lying down. Close your eyes and create this wonderful fantasy journey. Ignite the five basic senses along with the kinesthetic and affective as you travel, and feel yourself actively engaged in this setting.

Record the highlights of this experience. _____
_____
_____

What senses are dominant? _____
_____
_____

Which senses need strengthening? _____
_____
_____

Step 5. *Interpret the imagery (and unravel the puzzling symbolism).* Have you ever awakened puzzled by a dream? Suppose you dreamed that your house was on fire. Literally, this image might be reminding you to check the electrical wiring in your house. What else could this mean? More often than not, dream symbols are metaphorical. A dream of your house on fire could be a warning about an infection (fire) somewhere in your body (house). Interpreting puzzling symbols can be fun and is the detective portion of the Mindshift Method.

Amplification

With this first technique, you start with a central image and continue to free-associate until the real "Aha!" jumps forth. Let the stream of associations flow through without censoring any ideas. Put forth as many associations as you can. I love watching people while they are engaged in the amplification process. Their eyes always light up with the "I've got it" look when the intuitive connection is made.

Let's see how this technique works. Here's a question that involves a sudden onslaught of carpal tunnel syndrome. Sylvia does data entry work as an independent contractor. One day she begins making an unusual number of mistakes; she notices that her right thumb is feeling weak and a numbness is running up into her hand. The condition becomes so bad she can't complete her assigned work. She goes to the doctor and is diagnosed as having carpal tunnel syndrome. Sylvia is told to discontinue any kind of computer activity with her right hand. Concerned with the high volume of data entry that needs to be completed, she decides to use the Mindshift Method to help her with this dilemma. She poses the following question: "How can I complete my high volume of data entry work?"

To become centered, she stretches out on the floor and looks at the knots of wood on the ceiling. Then she concentrates on her breathing, takes several hang-sah breaths, and slowly visualizes herself relaxing. Starting at her feet, she works her way up her body until she reaches her torso, then through her neck, face, and scalp. When she asks her question, she sees two symbols: a clock face with illuminated hands and a musical note. Below are some of the amplifications she makes as she seeks to intuitively penetrate the meaning of these images.

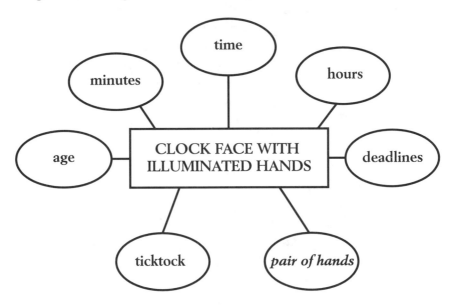

The "Aha!" came to Sylvia with pair of hands. Sylvia realizes she needs another pair of hands. To find out where the other pair of hands would come from, she turned to a second interpretation method.

Word Association

With word association, one word or thought triggers another until the real meaning or "Aha!" stands out. This creates a line of associations. Sylvia goes back to her second image—a musical note—

and applies the word association technique. She begins her train of associations: *musical note* → singing → choir → *Gloria*. The intuitive hit is Gloria, a member of her choir who has expressed a need for part-time work. Sylvia's insight is complete when she realizes that Gloria is computer literate. So just as Sylvia used this Mindshift process to resolve the dilemma created by her health condition, she can also use it to find a remedy for the condition itself.

PRACTICE: INTERPRETATION PRACTICE

Formulate a question about a health-related issue. Now become centered and receptive in order to elicit relevant imagery. Decipher the imagery by using the amplification technique. Then use word association to clarify that interpretation.

Question: _____

Amplification: _____

_____

_____

Word association: _____

_____

_____

Step 6.   *Rest.* Sometimes our mind is too tired to unravel our intuition's often puzzling imagery. When the intuitive insight is delayed and the interpretation is not apparent, you need to incubate the matter in your subconscious mind. While you are keeping your mind busy with other activities, intuitive insights may appear spontaneously. You might even find the answer coming in a dream or a reverie.

Step 7.   *Further examine the responses.* I find that intuitive responses to our questions often stimulate more questions. Consider the following dilemma. A woman who had been menopausal for ten years wondered about taking an estrogen replacement. She equivocated about this decision for months and grew weary from listening to arguments pro and con. Then she used the Mindshift Method, hoping her inner physician could resolve her dilemma. The image of an Easter bunny came hopping through her mind. Her associations revealed words such as "holiday," "rabbit," and "procreation," and then the image of an egg. The egg signified a new beginning. The intuitive mind then raised a whole host of other questions. To help her answer the question "When should I start taking the supplements?" she imagined a bar graph, which highlighted the third week. Then she wondered, "Will this interfere with the vitamins I am already taking?" She brought the image of a traffic light into her inner mind and immediately saw a green light. Notice how each question was answered in turn by eliciting the imagery and then interpreting the symbolism the imagery invoked.

Step 8. *Implement a solution.* This is the time when the logical mind comes forth to act upon the information provided by the intuitive mind. Our menopausal woman in the last example discovered that she could begin taking an estrogen replacement in three weeks.

Let's get back to Sylvia. After she did the Mindshift Method, her day was so filled with events, conversations, and meetings that there was little time to call Gloria. That evening, however, she did call Gloria—who was relieved to have the opportunity for part-time work. Gloria responded to a very relieved Sylvia by saying, "I can start tomorrow."

The Mindshift Method yields effective solutions to a person's health dilemmas. These solutions and the imagery through which they appear are unique to each individual, yet are available to all in the intuitive realm.

Chapter Three

OPTIMAL HEALTH IS AN INSIDE JOB

G ood health is an inside job!" What this means to me is that any health challenge can be resolved by tapping the wisdom from within and not just popping the pill from without. As Hippocrates, the father of medicine, said, "Natural forces within us are the true healers of disease."

How do you hear the wisdom coming from the inner physician? The answer comes from Key 4 in Chapter 1, which reminds us, "The intuitive mind speaks in pictures, symbols, and images." In this chapter, you will learn how to decipher the inner physician's guidance encoded in the pictures and images lodged in your imagination. Eliciting these images and unraveling the symbolism is also an inside job.

EMPOWERING INNER GUIDANCE

Using one's inner guidance to extract wisdom about the body's well-being can be far more accurate than results from a lab. And doctors as well as patients would do well to listen to it. I was touched by a case related by Dr. Deepak Chopra in his book *Creating Health*.[1] He had a patient named Anna who received a negative skin biopsy report and consequently felt quite agitated. Her distress immediately earned her a lecture from the attending physician, not consolation.

Days later, the embarrassed physician called to say that the lab re-ports had been mixed up. Anna did indeed have a rare type of cancer. She had an operation and was pronounced cured. But her inner phy-sician shouted out a warning, and she responded to the pronounce-ment with disbelief. This concern was puzzling to others, especially when the attending physician pronounced her whole and well. But she insisted that the data on her case be forwarded to an authorita-tive cancer clinic. There, the doctor confirmed Anna's suspicions: there was evidence of malignancy. Anna's intuition, her inner phy-sician, was right.

As Anna's case demonstrates, if doctors and health practitioners would listen to their patients, there would be fewer medical errors. This case reflects the theme echoed throughout this book, that in-dividuals can become their own best medical authority by relying on the wisdom of intuition.

As stories like Anna's reflecting mistakes in diagnosis multiply throughout the country, it is refreshing to read about Dr. Christiane Northrup, a caring physician with a practice in Maine who is dedi-cated to teaching women how to listen to and respect their inner guidance. Author of the best-selling book *Women's Bodies, Women's Wisdom*, she is changing how women view their own health prob-lems and the way they are treated by doctors. Dr. Northrup en-courages her patients to use their intuition to gain insight into the emotional core issues underlying such frustrating female health problems as PMS, endometriosis, vaginitis, and eating disorders. She encourages women to use their "inner guidance," or bodily wisdom, to create perfect health so that they become active participants in their own healing. Dr. Northrup reminds her readers and patients that the key to healing and renewal is in honoring these messages communicated from the needs and desires of the body.

Just because Dr. Northrup's work focuses on women does not mean that women's intuition is superior to men's, or that women have exclusive access to intuition's encodings. Everyone has intuitive ability, and through it, a way to the wisdom of the subconscious. Dr. Northrup's work emphasizes the value of intuition, and she urges our left-brained medical culture to acknowledge and respect this inside source of information.

JUST IMAGINE

The healing energy is not an outer pill but an inner power. It starts from deep within and reaches out beyond the boundaries of the physical body. You have all the tools, resources, techniques, and talent within you to heal many ailments, and even to help heal others. One of your tools, for example, is a fine imagination. Did you know that you can call on it to help you design a personalized health-care program? Albert Einstein sang the praises of imagination when he said, "Imagination is more important than knowledge. For knowledge is limited, whereas imagination embraces the entire world, stimulating progress, giving birth to evolution." Although everyone has an imagination, you alone are privy to your own imaginary realm. This is like having the key to a secret garden that only you are privileged to enter. The pictures in your imagination are seeds that can be planted in a field of dreams to help you bring into being your hopes and desires. Part of this manifesting includes creating elixirs and healing balms to cure any malady. This all happens when you use your wonderful faculty of imagination to communicate with your inner physician.

The practices in this chapter are intended to stoke the fires of your imagination, which can become a powerful tool to help you diagnose an ailment. The images in your head themselves contain the power to heal, repair, and restore. A student handed me a quote from Bob Rosen, the president of the Healthy Companies Group, which says, "People who can visualize the future often turn it into reality." I remember reading about a group of senior citizens who were interviewed to find out why they had remained vital and active, even into old age. They were found to have one thing in common. They had always *believed* they would live long and stay healthy.

People often invalidate the power of the mind by saying, "That's not real—it's just your vivid imagination." Sometimes it is difficult to distinguish the products of a vivid imagination from reality. For example, a University of Chicago experiment demonstrated how using the imagination led to extraordinary results. Three groups of students, none of whom were basketball players, were tested on their ability to shoot basketballs through a hoop. The first group was tested on their ability to shoot baskets from the foul line and then told to go home, forget about the test, and come back in thirty days.

The second group was also tested, then told to practice shooting baskets for an hour each day for the next thirty days. And the third group was also tested and then told to imagine shooting baskets for an hour each day for the next thirty days.

Who do you think had the greatest improvement in shooting baskets after thirty days: the group who did nothing special, the group that actually practiced, or the group that practiced in imagination only? The results were interesting. The people in the first group who did not practice had no change in their ability to shoot baskets. The second group who tried to better their record through actual practice improved by 24 percent. And the third group, those who merely *imagined* shooting baskets, improved by 23 percent. This study shows that a vivid imagination can produce real, measurable results. In fact, visualization is now standard for innumerable world-class athletes.

Now consider this: Any time an idea or thought comes to you, you get a mental image of it as well. Even if you're someone who believes you have no imagination or you can't visualize, subliminal pictures and images are continually arising from your inner mind. Every human being has a vivid imagination. Quantum physicians and body/mind therapists have made us aware of the mind's presence in every cell of the body. Each cell has a mind of its own, and can—and does!—signal to you when an area of the body is breaking down or is already in disrepair. This tightly knit connection between body and mind allows every cell in the body to change according to your thoughts and corresponding pictures.

This quantum viewpoint is becoming well accepted. You will note that every book listed in the back of this book underscores the theme that thinking positive, life-affirming thoughts will create a healthy, strong body. For example, imagine that this smiley face ☺ is pasted in every cell of your body. Take a moment to visualize this. How could anything go wrong with that image implanted in your mind and circulating through your body? You can learn to implant other positive images in your mind and body through the power of your imagination. The exercises in this chapter will help you identify and use the images in your head. By the time you read the last page of this book, you should be able to picture yourself radiantly healthy and free from limiting aches, pains, and irritations, and to believe that this image will blossom forth into reality.

Activating Your Imagination

If you are like most people, your capacity to use your imagination lies somewhere between those who claim they have no imagination and those whose imaginations run wild. If this is so, you'll have times when inspiring images readily appear in your mind to help you create, for example, a more interesting approach to a health challenge. The woman who is having difficulty breathing, for example, can imagine little elves sweeping away the debris inside her lungs. There may also be times when you draw a blank and can't imagine anything. Whether you consider yourself imaginative or not, be assured that you do have an imagination of limitless potential, and by stoking the right inner fire, you can retrieve images continuously.

Having taught the cultivation of intuition to countless people over the years in classes, seminars, and workshops, I've found that many people who resist connecting with their intuitive mind think of themselves as die-hard "logicals," incapable of imagining. Yet as I helped them connect with the pictures in their mind, they did recall moments of boredom or fatigue when they drifted off. They realized that during these daydreams, they had seen pictures and images as they fantasized about hunting in the woods, hooking the big one while fishing, taking shopping trips, or dancing on a moonlight cruise. Retreats into fantasy are always accompanied by images. Do you get the picture?

Remember the woman who was having difficulty breathing and imagined little elves sweeping away the debris inside her lungs. Can you imagine that scene? If not, let's arouse *your* imagination with this exercise designed to help you connect with a pleasant memory, which can be a favorite pastime or a sporting trip. Whether you realize it or not, all thoughts are attached to pictures. Our intent here is to capture and acknowledge those pictures.

PRACTICE: STALKING YOUR IMAGINATION

The first rule is not to try too hard. You can ignite the flow of ideas without effort. First sit in a comfortable place where you will not be disturbed. Then close your eyes and recall scenes evoked by the following suggested situations. Focus on one scene at a time and record the images that accompany it before proceeding to the next. Remember, you may not actually *see* images or pictures, but you will sense and experience them in your own characteristic way. Images arise automatically with every memory you recall.

Recall a place you really enjoyed visiting. Is it a lake, a park, a museum? As the memory surfaces, what pictures arise in your mind's eye? Record these images as fully as possible. _____

_____

_____

Recall a fun time with a family member. Where were you? What were you doing together? Record the images you receive. _____

_____

_____

What do you like to do in your spare time? A sport? Travel? Window shopping? Record your images. _____

_____

_____

_____

Write a sentence or two describing your experiences connecting with these images. For example, were these images easy to retrieve, moderately accessible, or difficult to access? Did you see them clearly? Were they vague or murky? Did you more sense them than see them? _____

_____

_____

_____

Creative Imagery

The imagination is a potent resource for healing physical maladies. Many doctors encourage their patients to engage in creative imagery regularly to accelerate their healing. Dr. Stephanie Simonton, one of the pioneers in working with creative imagery and immune enhancement, is well known for the research she conducts at the Arkansas Cancer Research Center. She has found that patients who were taught relaxation/visualization techniques showed a significant increase in immune responsiveness.

Dr. Dean Ornish is another researcher who is well known for his pioneering work in reversing atherosclerotic heart disease. His studies are described more fully in his well-known book *Dr. Dean Ornish's Program for Reversing Heart Disease*. His patients engage in a program of lifestyle changes, including meditation, visualization, dietary changes, and exercise. As one facet of this program, they learn to visualize their coronary vessels as clear and open. Cardiovascular fitness measures validated that adopting these lifestyle changes was instrumental in reversing coronary atherosclerosis.

When creative visualization came into vogue, many people learned how to create images or pictures in order to heal cancer and treat other health challenges. I knew a woman with severe arthritis who took to her rocker to rock her cares away as she visualized her painful, swollen joints being lubricated by a healing balm coming from a gold watering can. She watered these sore joints several times a day. Six weeks later, her doctors were astounded as they watched her hands and legs move freely and without pain. I prefer the term "creative imagery" to the more familiar term "creative visualization" in deference to those past and present students who cannot close their eyes and see, yet can comprehend imagery presented in other ways. For example, you may not see a gold watering can when you close your eyes, but in your imagination you can sense it is there.

You too can successfully consult your inner physician to find out what imagery you can use to rectify any health complaint. You will also be delighted to retrieve insights that can help your friends and associates.

Living in New York City taught me all about parking in tight spaces. I discovered that if you can get *into* a tight parking spot, you can get *out*. And metaphorically, when that tight spot we get into is deteriorating or poor health, it *does* have an out into a significantly improved condition. Once you recognize the tight space you are in, your inner physician can show you how to move out.

Months ago, I attended a creative imagery group. In addition to manifesting health for themselves, we all came together to don our super-health-sleuth caps. Everyone there knew that good health is an inside job. In this case, we had come to retrieve the images that would help return another person with a major ailment to optimal health.

The case presented was that of Jorge, a vibrant, loving, middle-aged man described by a relative as never having a bad word to say about anyone. To everyone's surprise, this man was now being pre-pared for major surgery. The group, not knowing any details about the case, became quiet. Each participant ascended to an inner di-agnostic chamber in order to connect with an inner physician and scan for trouble spots.

Then someone called out, "It's in the chest area." I added, "I see a broken heart." The leader confirmed our impressions and, praising our accuracy, revealed that Jorge would be having heart surgery shortly. We speculated about what body/mind forces had caused his health to deteriorate. Jorge had recently lost his job. Could this have led to the broken heart? But more important than our diagnostic skills was a group exercise we did together, imaging Jorge completely healed and resuming his daily activities. He was smiling, dancing, and receiving a letter offering him a new job. We even went into the future and imagined Jorge engaged in a job he loved.

This group is representative of similar groups that have formed all over the country. The people in attendance are taking responsi-bility for their well-being by attracting the cures and conditions that will maintain or restore optimum health and wellness.

Back to the Imaginary Garden

In the first exercise in this chapter, we began kindling your imagi-nation by arousing pictures or images that were associated with treasured moments. This was to introduce you to or remind you of the images that frequent your mind. The next three exercises will activate your imagination even more. Visualizing objects, activities, or processes is essential in creating your healing scenario. In the next exercise I will ask you to close your eyes, picture some objects, and set them into motion. Finally, you will create imagery to help restore an ailing area to wholeness. Remember, every thought has a picture attached to it. The focus of this exercise is learning how to identify these pictures in your inner mind—pictures most people take for granted.

Let's begin this series with something very basic: focusing on an object. Pick up a pen. Gaze at it as if you are seeing it for the first time. Notice details like the lines at the bottom of the pen, the shiny clip, and the color. Let any association to this pen surface. Do you remember the last time you used it? Do you remember who used it last? What does the surface feel like?

Now shut your eyes. Can you still see or imagine or sense this pen in some way? Notice what stands out. When you close your eyes, for example, does the color jump out at you?

PRACTICE: ELICITING A FAMILIAR IMAGE

Start this exercise by finding an object that you can hold in your hand: a stapler, teacup, fork, water bottle, or Scotch tape dispenser. Give this object your concentrated attention. Notice all the details individually, as well as your overall impression. Continue to pay attention to all the facets. Notice how your senses speak to you. Look at the object for a few minutes and then close your eyes. Let the image of this bubble up in your inner mind. Do you see it clearly with your eyes closed? How do you apprehend this object with any of your other senses? Do you feel it? Hear it? Smell it? Taste it? Sense it? Record your experience with this object.

The object of focus is _____

_____

What stands out about this object is _____

_____

_____

Memories associated to this object are _____

_____

_____

_____

When I close my eyes and think of this object, I experience ____

_____

_____

_____

_____

Getting Another Picture

Let's continue to ignite your imagination by having you look at another object. This time you will not have the actual object in front of you. Instead, you will notice what bubbles up in your mind as you picture an object I will suggest.

PRACTICE: IMAGINING THE BIG PICTURE

Before you start this exercise, select one of the following images to evoke your imagination or inner mind: a house, tree, broom, or cat. The object should not be in your sight. You can do this exercise with your eyes open or closed. Notice how you experience this object. After you "view" your object of choice, take the next step of setting it into motion. For example, you might see or sense a broom. Then imagine that the broom is sweeping away cobwebs. Then you might recall the sweeping brooms in the movie *Fantasia*.

The object of focus I chose is _____

_____

What stands out about this object is _____

_____

_____

What sensory experiences did you have of this object? _____

_____

_____

When I close my eyes and think of this object, I experience ____

_____

_____

What related memories were triggered? _____

_____

_____

I put the object in motion by imagining it _____

_____

_____

_____

Creating Healing Imagery

The more you work with your imagery, the stronger it will get. Our purpose is to strengthen this imagery so you can call upon your inner physician when needed to help you circumvent or mend a health crisis. For example, Janis's right knee still throbs from a fall she took eight months ago. It has stubbornly resisted healing through these agonizing months because she cannot take time out from work or personal responsibilities to rest it. Finally, she created the following imagery and her knee healed completely after three months.

As she closed her eyes and let her inner physician guide her inside this knee area, she sensed or saw the inflamed capillaries in her mind's eye. Her eyes still closed, in her imagination she took a special vial and poured drops of a golden liquid into the inflamed area and rubbed them in. Her knee was swollen and seemed to be engorged with water. So she imagined her knee to be sweating droplets that formed a little stream pouring from her knee.

Now, in this next exercise, let's create imagery to help restore an ailing area to wholeness.

PRACTICE: CREATIVE HEALING IMAGERY

Sit in a comfortable space in your Mindshift area. Become aware of a weak area or infirm spot in your body. How can you use imagery to show something happening to this area to restore it to wellness? For example, you might see an angel or elf come with a healing balm and rub it into the painful area. Or if your stomach feels tied up in knots, imagine you are untying each knot until the pain disappears. Be as fanciful as you like. You can always come back to this exercise later on to embellish your visualization.

What area of the body did you choose? _____
_____

What creative imagery did you use? _____
_____
_____

What did you notice? _____
_____
_____

How is that area now, six weeks later? _____

_____

_____

By engaging in creative imagery, you are generating and maintaining optimal health. Further, you are joining the ranks of people all over the world who are increasingly becoming holistic and proactive in caring for their health. As the cost of health care grows ever greater, many of us have noticed a paradigm shift, or change in values, taking place in the health industry. People must assume more responsibility for their well-being because the government will not pay to take care of them anymore. I have noticed in my professional practice that as people become increasingly informed about hazardous lifestyle "killer diseases," they become more focused on keeping themselves healthy and physically fit. By teaching you to consult your inner physician, this book gives you the opportunity to make the shift for yourself.

Imagery Does Work!

The following story shows how one man used creative imagery to accomplish a remarkable healing. Bob Gary, a retired CEO of Texas Utilities, focuses on the practice of thinking ourselves well, which is called neuropsychoimmunology. Bob strongly believes that with this method and good medical support, anyone can challenge diseases like polio and cancer and create a healthy life. He proved it by his own example, with the help of his inner physician.

At twenty-seven, Bob was a perfect physical specimen of a man. Then he contracted polio and was completely paralyzed for two years. Lying motionless in his hospital bed, he could do nothing but count the holes in the ceiling. Although this experience was devastating, Bob knew there must be some creative way to solve his problem. Listening to everything the doctors did and probing on his own, he intuitively realized that his brain was a more powerful tool than he had given it credit for being. He began to send signals from his brain to his muscles, to stimulate them so they wouldn't atrophy. Bob recovered after nine months of exercising his muscles with his mind and went on to officiate college football over the next thirty years.

Reflecting back on this encounter, Bob explained that though he seemed helpless, he knew that he could take the energy of his mind and apply it to his problem. Knowing that the brain is underused and has more power than we give it credit for, he mentally stimulated his body from within while the hospital staff worked on him from without. For example, while a staff member exercised him in the tub or a therapist helped him on the machines, Bob simultaneously exercised the muscles with his mind. He worked on himself continually, imagining in his mind the body he wanted to have in real life. And he got the muscles, limbs, and body, thanks to the intuitive healing power of his inner physician. Do you get the picture?

THE INTERNAL GOVERNING BOARD

The body/mind connection is irrefutable. You don't suddenly become sick because your body is run down, you sat next to someone with a cold, or you are being punished for something you did. Much evidence supports the notion that your thoughts, beliefs, and actions can catapult you into illness. Yet the mind that can make you sick can also make you well.

Your move to wellness can be accomplished with the help of the four quadrants of your inner being—body, mind, heart, and soul—the members of your internal governing board. When each of these partners communicates without interference, a sense of harmony results and you feel totally aligned and balanced. An appropriate phrase for this sense of completeness is *holistic health*.

These quadrants of your inner being can be likened to four executives who attend regular meetings to assess what is working or what is amiss in their organization. The organization, of course, is you, and the big four meet and communicate their findings to you by giving you a nudge in the form of a toothache, a headache, a feeling of depression, or a sense of disconnectedness from your life's purpose.

I have given new names to the members of my internal governing board honoring the function that each regulates. I call my body, which is aligned with the physical, by the name "Beautiful." Mental activities come under the jurisdiction of my mind, which I've named "Masterful." The heart, covering my emotional space, I like to refer to as "Healing." The spiritual quadrant, my soul, I call "Spirited."

These terms personify the ideal qualities I wish each member of my quadrant to embody. And I call upon my team to tell me what aspects of my life need to be attended to when I feel unbalanced. I join in the board meeting attended by Beautiful body, Masterful mind, Healing heart, and Spirited soul to learn the causes of and cures for my disconnectedness. I did this two years ago after a brief bout with a mild depression. I felt the pain that Kahlil Gibran calls "the bitter pill of the inner physician." My footing in the world slipped when the job I had had for three months as the director of development of an organization ended. In addition to that disappointment, I was incredibly fatigued due to an exhausting cross-country move and many stressful events of the previous year. I wondered what was causing the constant welling up of tears in my eyes.

When I visited my inner board of governors, I discovered that my Spirited soul had become so flattened that it needed a huge shot of prana, or life energy. The soul quadrant needed to be realigned with my other functions. With my soul dysfunctional, I had little physical energy and my heart was heavy. My disconnected soul affected my emotions and body. After this board meeting, guided by my inner physician, I was led to buy Joan Borysenko's book *Fire in the Soul*. What a perfect antidote for my darkness to find this book, which addressed the awakening of the soul from despair to optimism.

I participated in my board meeting each day by closing my eyes and imagining the five of us sitting around a table. I would pose a question and hear a reply in the recesses of my mind, which I recorded on a pad of paper. This was truly inner wisdom. The board emphatically said, "You need to start writing again!" I listened to this sage advice and within two weeks noticed the sunshine coming through the window and back into my heart. As I continued to write this book, passion was reawakened in my soul. I was writing about *Intuitive Healing*.

Connecting the Dots

The other day a friend called to tell me that she needed a healing and asked me to pray for her. This friend, in her mid-forties, is a highly successful administrator of a health-care facility. Her doctor had unduly alarmed her by saying she had very high blood pressure and was on the way to a heart attack if she didn't take steps to lower her blood pressure. I might add that this diagnosis fueled much agitation and fear. Listening carefully, I heard the word "heart" jump out at me, and I said, "Do you think this is related to a disappointment in your love life?" My friend has been in and out of a relationship with the same man for years and longs for commitment. She then realized that her highly elevated blood pressure was more connected to her aching heart than to the irritations at work. After realizing she was harboring images of herself as an old maid, she began to picture herself with a special suitor in her life. Can you see how this body/mind connection works? It is like the game of connecting the dots. When these dots are connected, you get the complete picture.

Three of the people attending one of my Intuitive Healing seminars expressed the following ailments. Lucy had a gum problem, Janis, whom you read about earlier, was rubbing her throbbing knee, and George was suffering pain in his left eye. Let's now try to figure out what the body/mind connection was telling each of these individuals. For example, Lucy's gums may reflect her keeping her mouth shut during times when she needs to speak out. Her mind says, "Grit your teeth, hold your words," and her mouth obeys, with painful results. Janis's knee stubbornly resisting healing may be telling her to stay in place for a while and not venture forth into any new terrain. Also, as the knee's function is to bend, she may need to be more flexible in life or relationships. George might wonder what he is not seeing clearly. He is unhappy at work but reluctant to change jobs. He feels his situation at work will improve but obviously doesn't see how destructive it is to his well-being. At the seminar, others encourage him to leave the job behind, which will truly effect a healing.

Now, it is your turn to examine what body/mind connections need to be unveiled so you can continue to improve and heal.

PRACTICE: CONNECTING THE MIND AND BODY

Find one or more bodily areas that are aching. Become still, go within, silently speak to each body part that needs healing, and ask to be shown the *real* underlying problem. Notice any imagery that arises. Discover what is out of phase in your mind, heart, or soul. Record these connections. Revisit this page frequently to add other insights about what you need to do for a complete healing.

Body Ailment _____ Out-of-Phase Quadrant

_____

The internal message is _____

_____

_____

_____

Body Ailment _____ Out-of-Phase Quadrant

_____

The internal message is _____

_____

_____

_____

Body Ailment _____ Out-of-Phase Quadrant

_____

The internal message is _____

_____

_____

_____

A COMMITMENT TO HEAL

Healing begins with the positive belief that you can be healed! This belief too is an inside job. I love the line from the hymn: "Only believe, only believe, all things are possible, only believe." A year and a half ago, I succumbed to despair after a periodontist told me I had bone loss under my gums that could never come back. A dentist had made this pronouncement, and I thoroughly believed it. Fortunately, my friend Dr. Karen Kramer, an adept body/mind practitioner, reminded me that anything is possible if you stay positive. That support helped strengthen my belief in the power of my healing energies. I instituted the following practice with my gums. Several times a week, I visualize my gums becoming healthier and the bone growth improving significantly. To complement this creative imagery practice, I visit my dental hygienist for a cleaning three times a year. In the eighteen months since that dire pronouncement was made, gum surgery has not been necessary, and according to my dental hygienist, some bone growth has taken place.

The relief that accompanies defying doctors' dire pronouncements always reminds me of Dr. Bernie Siegel's books,[2] which contain tales of many folks who challenged their doctor's advice when they were told they had a limited time to live. I recall the gardener who was given six months to live but went on for years after that edict "because he couldn't take the time to die." He had too many people counting on him to care for their lawns. Before you lock yourself into the "it can't be done" mentality, spin yourself around as a reminder that you can turn any challenge for healing around. And have a good laugh at this line from Oscar Wilde's play *The Importance of Being Earnest:* "The doctor said that Bunbury could not live, so Bunbury died." So much for paying attention to your physician!

Commit to Yourself

Your commitment to be healed begins with the belief that anything is possible. What do you want to heal? You don't need a gifted medical intuitive or doctor to tell you if you have an obvious medical challenge, such as a stiff neck, pain in the wrist, or heartburn. Undetected maladies, however, become obvious by means of a body scan. Later, we will practice doing a body scan. For now, let's focus on the obvious aches and pains. I now invite you to make a commitment to be healed.

PRACTICE: MAKING A COMMITMENT

Allow fifteen minutes for this practice. Go to your Mindshift area and sit in a comfortable chair or on the floor with your eyes open or closed. Review your bodily ailments, starting at your head and systematically traveling down your body as you note any health condition or irregularity in any bodily part that you want healed. Then feeling the power of your intention and the life force filling you, sign your name, and date this declaration.

HEALING DECLARATION

I declare that I can actualize a healing for myself with respect to these conditions: _____

_____

_____

_____

   Name _____ Date _____

   Activated by your commitment, your inner physician will be showing you how to restore these ailing areas to a vibrant state of health. This will become especially apparent as you become more adept at using the Mindshift Method.

Chapter Four

THE HEALING WISDOM
OF THE DREAM

In the last chapter you learned how to access the vast storehouse of the subconscious, using the Mindshift Method to elicit and interpret imagery that provides diagnoses and remedies, insights and new perspectives to guide you on the path of healing. But in fact we enter that intuitive realm of potent imagery each night, in the natural Mindshift state of dreaming. In this chapter, you will learn to elicit dreams, unravel their symbolic language, and recognize the healing wisdom imagery they contain.

LISTENING TO THE WISDOM IN YOUR DREAMS

The life and theories of renowned psychiatrist Carl Jung were significantly shaped by the messages bubbling up from his dreams. He said, "The dream is an invaluable commentator and illuminator of life. Listen to the wisdom of the dream." Your inner physician's voice calls to you each night in the symbolic imagery of your dreams.

You can go into the Land of Nod and retrieve incredible healing insights. Your inner physician, speaking through a dream, can foreshadow health challenges, illuminate their meaning in your life, diagnose and prescribe treatments, and even chart the course of your illness, letting you know when your recovery is complete.

I hope this chapter, a brief stroll through the field of dreams, will inspire you to become more intensely involved in dream study. Among the many wonderful books on dream interpretation is Dr. Patricia Garfield's *Healing Power of Dreams*.[1] She says, "Your dreams can help keep you healthy, warn you when you are at risk, diagnose incipient physical problems, support you during physical crises, forecast your recuperation, suggest treatment, heal your body, and signal your return to wellness. All this becomes available to you each night as you learn to use the healing power of your dreams." Two other excellent books on healing and dreams are Joan Windsor's *Dreams and Healing* and Robert Trowbridge's *The Hidden Meaning of Illness—Disease as a Symbol and Metaphor*.

Earlier in this book, I mentioned how a dream in which a doctor misdiagnosed me with cancer prepared me for a real-life event that occurred months later. Thanks to this dream alert from my inner physician, I knew my doctor was wrong when he insisted I have an operation to remove a "cancerous growth." Heeding my inner physician helped me avoid needless and costly surgery! Ever since that time, I have felt confident that my inner physician would send a warning in the event of something serious. My wise inner guide, and yours, can also provide healing perspectives, as you can see from the next dream.

Two years ago I moved to California from the Midwest. Although physically exhausted by the move, I immediately resumed a ten-hour workday that soon took its toll on my health. My poor body cried out for tender loving care through one ache and pain after another. I finally asked my inner physician to let me know if I needed serious medical attention. The following dream came days later.

STOPPING THE INTRUDER

Jim, my husband, and I went out for a walk. Then I met Mel Hardy, an old beau I hadn't seen in years. He wanted me to go out with him, but I said I had to get back to Jim. Next I met another old beau, Joel Lieber, but I didn't talk to him. Then I was going to my father's Pine Street office. Someone was following me and I felt frightened. I went in and bolted the door so the person couldn't get into the waiting room. I was nervous at first, but then felt safe.

The inner physician speaks in a dream language whose revealing images never cease to amuse me. Dream symbols seem to be plucked from a vast computer database in the subconscious realm. Now my dream provided clues in the form of two former beaus, Mel Hardy and Joel Lieber, one of whom I hadn't seen in eighteen years and the other for nearly forty! Why did my inner physician pick them to symbolize my current health concern? Then I saw the puns in their names. When someone is hardy or hearty, they are healthy and strong. The word *Lieber* in German means love and vitality. So in the first part of my dream I am turning away or rejecting health and vitality.

Information about my childhood is needed to understand the next part of the dream and perceive the healing motif within. My father, a noted Philadelphia cardiologist, had an office on Pine Street. My nervousness about being followed is analogous to being stalked by an illness. In the dream, I go into the doctor's waiting room and bolt the door against the intruder; then I feel safe. This is showing me that if I take precautions—bolt the door against illness—I can safely wait for my health to return. This dream left me feeling reassured, and after I followed its symbolic advice, my health and vitality soon returned.

Now, let us explore further the landscape of dreams.

DREAM PRIMER

This is a brief primer of dreams. For an expanded version, see my *Intuition Workbook*. Since the language of dreams is metaphoric or symbolic, look for the underlying meaning of the images. Dreams often use puns to communicate. In my dream, for example, Hardy and Lieber referred to my vitality and health, and in figuring out why I responded to these characters in my dream as I did, I realized dream interpretation is like detective work. The images contain clues needed to unravel the mystery. Occasionally the symbolic images are nearly impenetrable. Sometimes a dream is so literal that what you dream is what you get. A very important canon of dream interpretation is that the symbol belongs to you, as it was sent by your subconscious mind. Only *you* can say with finality what a dream symbol really means.

In the weekly dream group I attend, we help each other untangle the symbolism in our dreams. The dreamer first free-associates. Then each of us offers his or her insights and interpretation, first saying, "If this were my dream symbol, this is what it would mean to me." Each person will see symbolic associates to parts of the dream that others may miss. The insights of a group are an invaluable resource for dream interpretation. Here is a portion of a healing dream that I had, followed by the group's interpretation.

THE RELEASEMENT

I was walking up a long flight of stairs to the top of the Tower. Mom was following behind. This was at the Hotel Pierre in New York City. At the top we had to sign into a guest book. I saw Steve Novosel and went back to look in the guest book and noticed I had also been there in 1986. I showed Steve the book. Mom was sitting next to me and the program was about to begin. There was a woman I knew, wearing a white face mask. We were given an exercise and had to release something. I looked over at Steve and noticed he was wearing a hearing aid and looked like Grandpa Paul.

I was puzzled by the symbolism in this dream, so my group helped me with the probe. Ann wanted to know what happened in 1986. I search my memory for what major or minor event happened in that year. I suddenly realized that my beloved mother died in 1986. Since she was behind me in the dream, I now realize my grieving for her is truly behind me. Jay asks me what I think about the white face mask, which he feels is another interesting clue. In some cultures this is a death mask. To me, it symbolizes purity and newness. Aha! Just as my mother went through a physical transition, I too have to release something to go through a transition or become transformed. I wonder why an old friend, musician Steve Novosel, is presented. Another "Aha!" comes from Julia, who says, "Let's look at his name." She points out that *Novosel* can be broken down into nova cell, which then translates into new cells. How healing and regenerative to release an old pattern in order to create new cells and grow. Norma asks me to explore what I associate with Grandpa Paul. I tell the group that he lived in California for thirty-five years, right up until his death, and symbolized many things to me. The dream character named Steve, who looked like Grandpa Paul, was wearing a hearing aid. Haruko asks, "What have you not been listening to?" Stringing these associations together, I realize that since coming to California I have not been listening to what needs to be released so I can transform, grow, and regenerate in my new environment.

Not only are our dreams intriguing, but catching the right meaning can be a lot of fun! Now try interpreting some symbols yourself. Explore what they mean to you. By working with symbols in this way, you are learning the language your dreams use to speak to you.

PRACTICE: DECIPHERING SYMBOLS

What do these dream symbols suggest to you? Write down as many associations as you can. Remember that there are no right or wrong interpretations. The significance in a symbol is what it means to *you*, not to anyone else. When you finish, you can see my interpretations.

Cat _____

_____

_____

_____

House on fire _____

_____

_____

_____

Chest wound _____

_____

_____

_____

Having a baby _____

_____

_____

_____

Clown _____

_____

_____

_____

MARCIA'S INTERPRETATIONS

Cat: Aloof, mysterious, independent, hunter, graceful, feminine energy

House on fire: Warning to check home for fire hazards, someone burning you up, health condition (fever, infection)

Chest wound: Lack of confidence, heartache, heart condition, release of profound emotion

Having a baby: Creating something new, a new project, a new you

Clown: Playing a comic role to hide your true feelings, putting things in a different perspective, immature viewpoint, happy fool

Dreams Can Come Spontaneously or Upon Request

Our dreams are often spontaneous images arising from our subconscious in response to our unexpressed needs. They can even provide previews of upcoming events, foretelling accidents or impending calamities. "Coming events cast their shadows beforehand," Goethe said. And those shadows often take the form of dreams. But frightening dreams don't always mean what they most obviously suggest. One of my students had a vivid dream that his supervisor was in an automobile accident. He wondered if he should warn her to drive carefully. A car appearing in a dream can represent your body or your way of approaching situations in life. A car dream may be telling you to shift gears, to slow down or speed up. In exploring this dream about his supervisor, the student saw that she was working at a frantic pace and realized she was in danger of "crashing" if she didn't slow down. His dream embodied his unconscious awareness of his supervisor's self-destructive work habits.

While most dreams come unbidden, we can also make requests of our dreams and they will respond. As an experiment, ask your dreaming mind to respond to a specific question or issue and notice what happens. For example, you might ask your inner physician to send you a dream showing you how to heal your arthritic hand or what is the best treatment for your thyroid problem. (Make this request before sleep from the Mindshift state for maximum effectiveness.)

You can even program a dream about another person. Months after I moved to California, a friend who was concerned about my health requested dream information from her inner physician about my condition. In response, she had the following dream. In the dream, she saw me slumped over the wheel of a car. Literally, this seemed to imply I would be involved in a car accident. We delved beneath this outward appearance and saw the dream saying I was being a slouch and not in control of my own vehicle or body. The clear message was that I needed to take responsibility for my own health—not slouch on this job.

Catching a Dream

"Catch" a dream and practice your interpretation skills. Many students in my graduate course, Whole Brain Thinking for Managers: Integrating Intuition and Logic, claimed they didn't dream. I challenged them to suspend that assumption and "call" for one dream. And that one dream, when it came, set their dream factories to work. Everyone dreams. But if you are one of those people who don't remember, then call for one breakthrough dream. Then pay attention. It won't be long before you too catch a dream.

Try changing your attitude, replacing "I can't recall a dream" with "I can remember my dreams." Say "I can and will remember my dreams" to yourself again and again during the day. Then at night, keep a notebook and pen or cassette recorder by your bed so that as soon as you wake up you can record any dreams you have had. Before you go to sleep, give the suggestion to your dreaming mind that you will fall asleep quickly, sleep soundly, awaken feeling refreshed, and remember your dreams.

Voilà! The morning comes when you capture a dream. Now record it in your dream book. Be sure to date the dream. My practice is to record the date by entering the date of the day before as well as today's. Today my dream-book entry reads October 2/3, which tells me that the dream occurred somewhere between the night of the second and morning of the third.

INTUITIVE DREAM INTERPRETATION

Now analyze your dream. What does this reverie mean? Here are six steps to help you decode the underlying message in the dream.

1. *Give the dream a title.* Title the dream in eight words or less. Titles capture the meaning underlying the dream.
2. *Underline the major symbols or concepts embedded in the dream.*
3. *Extract the theme.* In one sentence, describe the bottom line of the dream.
4. *Determine the emotional content of the dream.* The feelings at play in the dream are important clues.
5. *Use amplification and/or word association to analyze the most important symbols.*
6. *Integrate the logical and intuitive minds.* After your analysis, ask yourself: "What intuitive insights help me understand the dream message?" Then use your logical mind to figure out how to implement the intuitive information. If, for example, you lost your wallet in the dream, the intuitive mind might provide the insight that you lost your identification or self-esteem. Then the logical mind would suggest going to a support group to reclaim your identity.

When you have finished, you might want to capture any part of the dream with a drawing. This step may be left out but can help you understand the dream symbols.

A Sample Intuitive Dream Analysis

Let me walk you through the intuitive dream interpretation steps. Donna, one of my graduate students, consulted her inner physician, who directed her to join Weight Watchers. She had the following dream two weeks later, and analyzed it using the system modeled above. Here is each step of her analysis.

Title.   Time of Renewal

Imagery.   I was at a <u>bazaar</u> in South Haven and went to lunch with Vicki, Dorothy, and a man. I couldn't find a place to park because the street was under <u>construction.</u> We went into the <u>restaurant,</u> where they were also doing <u>renovation.</u> We finally found a <u>place to eat</u> in a <u>smaller dining room.</u> The meal was <u>cluttered.</u> There were lots of <u>things to buy.</u> A <u>planter</u> in the shape of a <u>hen with a hat (white with a green plant)</u> was on the table. I was thinking of buying it when <u>my mother bought it for me.</u> She was thinking of giving it as a gift to Dorothy, but <u>wanted me to have it instead.</u>

Theme.   Renovation related to eating and mothering, or nurturing.

Emotional Content.   Very upbeat, expectant, peaceful.

Amplification.   The word "renovation" jumps out at Donna. She amplifies to this symbol to find a key to the dream.

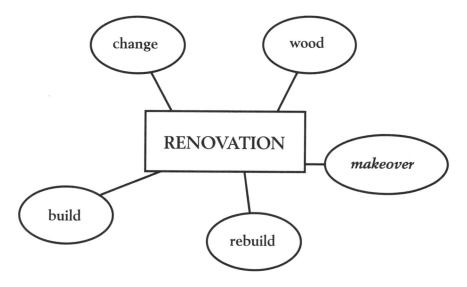

Implementation.   Donna feels like she is under reconstruction, seriously involved in a makeover with her participation in Weight Watchers. The reference to a smaller dining room is what she is doing by focusing on smaller dining habits. The green in the plant reinforces the theme of healing and growth and tells her that she is on the way to a healthier lifestyle. Finally, her mother rewards her efforts by giving her a gift, nurturing her just like a mother hen.

Here is an analysis of another graduate student's dream. This analysis underscores the necessity of not taking the dream at face value until the meaning of the underlying symbolism is explored. Shirley had an alarming dream about her mother's health. She wanted to understand the message embedded in this dream. This dream came weeks before Thanksgiving when Shirley and her husband were faced with the inevitable annual dilemma of deciding which family to visit for the holiday dinner. Before this dream occurred, they were leaning toward going to her husband's family for the holiday.

Title.   We Gather Together.

Imagery.   The <u>family was gathered together</u> for an event and was preparing to go somewhere. My <u>mother</u> was <u>not feeling well,</u> so we called a doctor. This <u>doctor was female</u> and explained that my mother had a <u>blood clot in her uterus</u> and <u>couldn't be moved.</u> We all knew we had to stay, but were getting ready to leave. We left her in the <u>lower level in the house</u> so that if someone came in while we were gone, they couldn't hurt her. She was on a <u>bed in the lower level</u> where she had been examined. My father discounted her unwellness. My <u>sister and her family</u> were there for the <u>holiday meal,</u> as well as some family friends, <u>Jack and Dorothy.</u>

Theme.   Caring for a sick mother.

Emotional Content.   No one was distraught or concerned, including my mother.

Amplification.   I was troubled by the blood clot even though the dream carried no sense of foreboding or of imminent danger. I free associate to the words ''blood clot.''

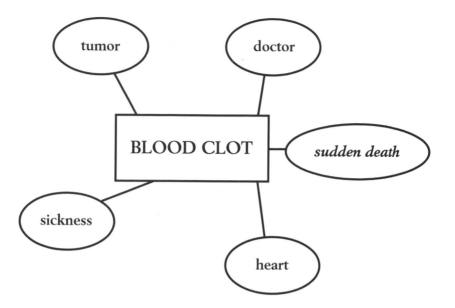

What stands out to my amplification are the words "sudden death." I want another insight to understand this, so I do a word association to the word "uterus."

uterus ⇒ children ⇒ love

Implementation.   The dream "Aha!" of sudden death reminds me of my mother's mortality and my love for her. This makes me want to find a way for us to spend a major part of the holiday together. This dream left me with a strong sense that we should go to my sister's home for Thanksgiving, since my parents would also be visiting.

Perhaps Shirley's mother wasn't in bad health in real life, but the dream is giving a clear warning that her health could have deteriorated if she didn't have the loving support of a visit from her family.

PRACTICE: USE YOUR DREAM INTERPRETATION SKILLS

Activate your intuitive dream interpretation skills. After recording a dream, write down what you did for each step of this analysis.

Title _____

_____

Imagery _____

_____

_____

_____

Theme _____

_____

Emotional content _____

_____

_____

Amplification _____

_____

_____

Implementation _____

_____

_____

HEALING IMAGERY

The following dream, taken from Dr. Bernie Siegel's book *Love, Medicine, and Miracles*,[2] shows how a diagnostic insight was retrieved through an image. A nurse who had been sick for weeks with an undiagnosed illness had the following dream:

> A shellfish opened, a worm stood up inside it, and an old woman pointed at the worm and said, "That's what's wrong with you."

From this brief dream, the nurse realized she had hepatitis, an infection of the liver. Consuming shellfish from tainted waters caused it. Her dreaming mind knew this and communicated to her in an explicit, literal image. Not surprisingly, subsequent tests confirmed the hepatitis.

Jill Gregory, founder and director of both the Novato Center for Dreams and the Dream Library and Archive, shares the following dream, which convinced her to obtain a needed surgery. Since age nineteen, Jill had suffered from occasional incontinence. Over the years, the condition worsened, but only gradually. Finally, Jill discovered there was no remedy other than surgery. She was so terrified of hospitals and operations, she refused the surgery. Then, in her early forties, she had the following dream.

THE LEAKING TOILET

I am living in a house with refugees from Vietnam. The house is barely adequate for our needs despite our efforts to keep it clean and do minor improvements, like yard work. The landlord never comes around to repair things and we try not to bother about problems that occur. While sitting in the living room, I notice water leaking from down the hall in the bathroom. The water is leaking out of the toilet, running down the hallway and into the living room. As I watch, I feel increasingly distressed. The water has taken up most of the living room floor! We can't ignore this! We need our living room. Someone has to call the landlord. The old matriarch of the Vietnamese family is quite insistent that the landlord must be called. I was the one who arranged for this rental and whose name is on the lease. I must call the landlord and insist that he get a plumber here to fix the leak. I wake up with a feeling of urgency and resolve.

Jill, an expert dreamworker, offers this interpretation of her dream. "This dream was my wake-up call about the leaking now being an urgent situation requiring a quick response by the tenant, the landlord, and the expert in repairing leaks—the plumber. The image of the living room being covered with water was a direct picture for me of how much of my room to live my life was affected by incontinence. In the dream I need to be the responsible tenant who brings the plumbing problem to the attention of the landlord. I realized that I was feeling distant from the 'landlord of my body' self who was empowered to make the executive decision about the proper response to the crisis. The character of the elderly matriarch embodied the attitude with which I needed to identify in order to make the phone call.

"As it turned out, the timing was excellent in that I had recently acquired adequate health insurance, my children were old enough to be relatively self-sufficient, and a dear friend who was staying with us at the time was able to help out by being there for the children as necessary. He was a needed support to us through this crisis. The dream also provided support in the form of a funny synchronicity. When I did actually go to the doctor's office for the official visit to finalize plans for the surgery, I heard a lot of unusual noises coming from a room next to my doctor's waiting room. The door was ajar, and when my curiosity got me to look in the room, I saw two plumbers noisily repairing the toilet in the bathroom!"

Dream Aphorisms

As an international authority on dreams and author of many dreams books, Dr. Patricia Garfield has amassed considerable information about the field of dreams. She recommends giving yourself a daily dream checkup to see if any dream characters are rigid or immobile, overactive or frenzied, or if any dream characters, including yourself, have a physical illness or infirmity. She is also careful to point out that a dream about any illness or dis-ease can be metaphorical, a representation of minute physical sensations, or a combination of metaphor and physical sensation. For example, if you dream about a deaf person, it might have one of the following meanings: you are not listening to someone; your hearing could be failing a bit; or you are not listening to the warning provided by your inner self to have your hearing checked.

PRACTICE: CREATING HEALING DREAMS

Now, to further familiarize yourself with dream symbolism, do the following exercise. Recall the last three physical ailments you have experienced. Now become your own inner physician and create a dream for each one. For the first ailment, do a warning dream. For the second, do a diagnosis dream, and for the third, do a prescription or remedy dream. Use the Mindshift Method to commune with your inner physician, in the relaxed, intuitive state, as you "create" the appropriate imagery for these dreams. This exercise will give you access to the healing process by increasing your understanding of dream interpretation.

Warning dream _____

_____

Diagnosis dream _____

_____

Remedy dream _____

_____

News from the Intuitive Dream Bulletin

As you become more confident about the messages you receive from the Land of Nod, you will look forward to any dream bulletin containing diagnoses or cures. Wouldn't it be wonderful to receive regular dream updates on your current physical condition, complete with recommendations? Here is a wonderful account of how a clinical psychologist used such dream bulletins to accelerate her healing journey.

Dr. Meredith Sabini specializes in dream consultation in her practice. In addition, she has published original research on dreams of illness and healing. Her interest in this area began in the 1970s when she was immersed in Jungian analysis and had a series of dreams about some lifelong problems. Although most of her own dreams focused on the psychodynamics and meaning of illnesses, there were occasional dreams that directly led to behavioral change. Dr. Sabini tells the following story of one such experience:

"For several years, I had been plagued by getting sick around the holidays; typically a virus or infection kept me in bed between Christmas and New Year's for at least a full week. Finally, one year, a dream in mid-November opened up the underlying meaning. Here is my dream:

> I dreamed of running into Jan, my former neighbor, whom I liked and missed. She tells me that she now has a good program—that she sleeps nine hours and no longer gets sick. It seems like a good idea.

"As I explored the dream in my analysis, it became evident that

Jan was an aspect of the psyche that had been absent and was returning. Jan, an actual body therapist and dancer, symbolized someone who was in touch with bodily needs and rhythms, someone I could learn from. She gave me the basic idea that more sleep was needed. The same night I dreamed I was telling someone the importance to Native Americans of shields. I told the person I need a shield and plan to make one."

Meredith acknowledges that these dreams and subsequent ones showed her that though on one level she liked the social activities during the holidays, on another she felt the need to retreat and be still. Meredith had been working against this basic pull to go into herself during winter, and her illnesses were an unconscious way of forcing her to obey this deeper urge.

Prompted by her dreams, she planned a retreat for that week. It was a turning point for both her health and her attitude about the cycles of nature. She made a shield for herself against the pull to manic activity and began to take more quiet time as well as sleep more. Her retreats became an important ritual, and she often took her dream journal and reflected on the year's material.

After engaging in this practice for several years, Meredith described the following rather humorous dream:

> I am at a table having a discussion with others. I mention that I hibernate for four to six weeks every winter and that around mid-December, I begin sleeping nine to ten hours per night. I also prefer to stay home rather than go out. The hibernation then ends, and my sleep cycle returns to eight hours. A man at the table is a rational type who tries to attribute this process to the intake of air or some similar outer, physiological explanation. I say, "No, it's just plain hibernation."

"With this dream, the process reached a completion. I now had a name for what was taking place—hibernation! And although an overly rational aspect of the psyche does not buy this, I am unperturbed and know that I am hibernating, just as animals do. Although initially I rested because of illness, I eventually learned to rest voluntarily, to enjoy the seasonal, psychic change. I made some adjustments in my personal and work life so that the shift could run its natural course; and I came to relish the experience of deep introversion and devotion that accompanied it."

Dreams Can Come Anytime

Your inner physician can visit you through a dream in the still of the night, in the midst of a daydream, during a catnap, or during a meditative state. Dr. Jean Slane, an assistant professor of family medicine at the University of Wisconsin, directs the Wiselives Center in Wauwatosa, Wisconsin. Dr. Slane is a family physician specializing in women's health and complementary medicine. Her main interest is in helping patients discover and maintain a sense of integrity and wholeness.

Dr. Slane spends time in "intentional" meditation for particular patients with difficult problems. On one particular occasion, she nodded off during meditation and received vital health information about an expectant mother. In her dream, the mother could no longer write from left to right, but wrote everything backward. And a dream "therapist" warned her that it would be dangerous if the mother were to write forward.

When she awoke, she realized that the dream related to the breech, or backward, birth she was anticipating in her patient. Her plan had been to externally rotate the baby in the womb so that it faced downward in the normal position. After discussing the dream with the expectant mother, she decided to allow a breech position delivery. The delivery went fine. After the delivery, the baby's great-grandfather told Dr. Slane he had had the *same* dream! In his dream, though, Dr. Slane was the therapist and the great-grandfather was the backward writer. It seems his inner physician confirmed her diagnosis with a second opinion!

Here is another example from Dr. Slane's dream archives of a dream as a warning. Dr. Slane dreamed about a patient who was pregnant. In the dream, the patient wore fishnet stockings white from the knees down and red above. The next morning, the patient called from out of state to say she had miscarried that night and awakened with a lap full of blood.

These prophetic or precognitive dreams are discussed more fully in my *Intuition Workbook*.

Dream Healing

There are times when the realm of the dream crosses a very fine line, into the realm of the supernatural. Norma DeArmond was quite alarmed when she woke around midnight with an excruciating pain in her chest. In a split second, she sensed that the room was filled with angels. She heard one of the angels tell her to reach for a pillow and place it under her back and head, which she did. The angel instructed her not to move but to remain in this elevated position. Quick as a flash, a huge angel dressed in a white suit, with straps crisscrossed across his chest, appeared and stood at her bedside. She was aware of the knot in her chest. This larger-than-life angel identified himself as a doctor and made some hand motions that helped Norma fall into a deep sleep. She awoke three hours later, completely healed.

When Norma recovered from this incredible healing ordeal, which she likened to a near death experience, she intuitively knew that the angel had come to save her life. Intuitively, Norma received the message from the angel that she was needed as a healing instrument to bring peace and comfort to family and friends. Norma was filled with indescribable peace and security. I was amazed when I saw her days later. I couldn't help but notice that she looked at least ten years younger. And I still wonder what, if any, difference there is between healing angels and our inner physician.

DREAM HELPER CEREMONY

The last part of this chapter focuses on dream sharing, or dedicating your dream to finding healing insights for others. This procedure, known as the dream helper ceremony, was created by Dr. Henry Reed and Dr. Bob Van de Castle. Both have been prolific participants in the field of dreams. Bob's most recent book, *Our Dreaming Mind,* is a sweeping exploration of the role that dreams have played in politics, art, religion, and psychology, from ancient civilizations to the present day. Henry's books include *Dream Solutions* and *Getting Help from Your Dreams.*

Some twenty years ago, Bob and Henry developed their dream helper ceremony in which they invited a group of people to seek dream solutions to another person's problem. In this process, the person in need of healing, the target person, acknowledges that a troubling emotional problem exists but does not give any information about the problem. The dream helpers take to their beds and sleep on it, requesting insight from their dreams to help the target person get a new perspective on the problem. Prior to falling asleep, the dream helpers strengthen their bonding with the target person by engaging in a ritual. They can meditate, pray together, and receive an object such as a piece of clothing or jewelry from the target person; this object can either be worn or placed by their bedside in order to deepen contact when in the dream state.

When the dream helpers gather the next morning, each in turn will share any dreams from the preceding night. A pattern begins to emerge as these dreams are considered and analyzed by the target person in light of his or her problem. Bob and Henry have been conducting dream helper ceremonies for the past twenty years. They are always impressed with the collective accuracy of the dream helpers in identifying problems and arriving at feasible solutions.

Here is an excerpt describing one of the ceremonies from *Our Dreaming Mind*:[3]

> The target woman's question, which she revealed after all the helpers' dreams had been reported, dealt with whether to enter some new, as yet undetermined, vocation. Almost every dream helper reported dreams of extreme violence: wild animals were involved, someone was hit on the head with a hammer, and other acts of aggression were mentioned. There were also several mother-daughter dreams with disturbing content; one had a mother duck and several drowned baby ducks. When I asked the target person why she thought there was so much violence in these dreams and why the troubled mother-daughter relationships were portrayed, she broke down and confessed that her mother, who had been a psychiatric patient, had been quite violent and cruel to her when she was younger. Her mother had once tried to drown her in a tub of boiling water, which helped explain the image of the drowned baby ducks. The subsequent group discussion suggested that maybe the target person needed to resolve this old issue with a therapist before moving on to a new vocation.

PRACTICE: BECOME A DREAM HELPER

I'd like to engage you in an adapted version of the dream helper ceremony, oriented toward another person's healing. For this practice, collaborate with three friends. One of you, the target person, should have a physical ailment for which a dream diagnosis or remedy is requested. The other three dream helpers will dedicate that evening's dream to the target person. The target person may or may not disclose the nature of the problem for which he or she is seeking guidance. As you gather together on the chosen evening, engage in some bonding activity. Here are additional directions from Bob's book. "Meditate, pray, sing together, or sit silently holding hands. It's useful if the target person can loan some personal object—jewelry, a photograph, or an article of clothing—to each dream helper. Wearing that object or having it by the bedside will enable each dream helper to feel a special connection with the target person when they go to sleep that evening."[4]

Record your dream about the target person. _____

_____

_____

_____

_____

_____

How was this related to the target person's concern? _____

_____

_____

_____

_____

What health insights, diagnoses, or remedies were suggested by your dream? _____

_____

_____

_____

The best way to end this chapter on dreams is to encourage you to start incubating and actively working with your dreams. Notice the excitement that results as you learn to access the healing wisdom of your dreams, from discovery to recovery, all the way to radiant health.

Chapter Five

THE INVIGORATING POWER
OF THE MINDSHIFT

MAY THE FORCE BE WITH YOU

We all have health challenges. They can be anything from hangnails, headaches, bruised knees, or congestion to major diseases such as cancer, AIDS, and TB. The stresses of life can wear down the immune system, making us vulnerable to accidents, illness, and disease.

In the past, when I felt overwhelmed by work or personal difficulties, I wished I could wave a magic wand and make all the pain and aggravation go away. But now that I regularly commune with my inner physician, I am never downhearted for long. Instead of feeling weak and ineffectual, I am now empowered by my inner physician, whose magic wand of intuition provides healing solutions to any dilemma.

Any negative health condition deprives us of the energy we need to function in top form. When we are sick, we don't have a lot of energy. The get-up-and-go may also leave us temporarily when we are at difficult points in our lives. This can also make us vulnerable to health problems. We then must revitalize ourselves physically and mentally and heal ourselves by addressing the root of the problem. This is where the inner physician and the Mindshift Method prove invaluable.

Before presenting the Mindshift Method in detail, let us briefly explore the body/mind connection. Body and mind are inseparably united. And every physical malady has symbolic or metaphysical implications. Finding an underlying meaning in an ailment points the way to healing. And the intuitive mind can locate this hidden information.

Mindshift to the Rescue

Whenever I hear people talk about their back going out of alignment or their troublesome knees, I'm amazed at their assumption that the problem is strictly physical. Remember, every health problem has symbolic implications and is in a sense a physical reflection of a nonphysical challenge. When your back, which supports you, goes out of alignment, you might ask yourself, "What facet of support is out of alignment in my life? And what can I do to take responsibility for it and for my own healing?"

By exploring physical ailments in this way, you will become more aware of this body/mind connection and of the symbolic nature of bodily distress. This knowledge will help you to engage in proactive holistic healing, rather than merely reactive symptom management.

My work with thousands of people in the area of intuition development and intuitive healing has given me many valuable insights into this process. Through my work I have learned how to apply the power of the intuitive mind to major and minor crises—physical, mental, and spiritual—in all arenas. The methods and practices I employ all derive their power from contact with the inner physician through the Mindshift Method. I will now lead you through the Mindshift process, by which you, too, can contact your inner physician. Below is an overview of the steps involved, all covered in earlier chapters. Using case story examples, I will illustrate each step so that its applications are clear.

THE MINDSHIFT METHOD:
A STEP-BY-STEP OVERVIEW

1. Issue.   Frame your issue, problem, or concern succinctly in the form of a question, such as "Why am I having chronic lower-back problems?"

2. Centering.   Release the mental tension by:

- Repeating an *affirmation*, such as "My inner physician directs me to the perfect healing solution."
- Using a *focusing word* or *phrase* to restore equanimity. You can say "serenity," "joy," or phrases such as "peace be still" or "I am in God's hands"—whatever gives you a feeling of comfort or peace.
- Focusing on a *geometrical object*, *picture*, or *pattern* to silence the verbal mind. You can also focus on a flower, the pattern in a rug, a meaningful object, or a soothing image or picture.
- Listening to soothing *music* (without lyrics).
- You can also combine any of these, perhaps repeating an affirmation while gazing at a picture and listening to soothing music.

3. Receptivity.   Release the physical tension by using:

- *Breathing techniques*, including the hang-sah and total breaths.
- *Relaxation practices*, including the tense-and-release technique and the count-down exercise.

4. Imagery.   Elicit pictures, symbols, or imagery from the intuitive mind.

5. Interpret the Imagery.   Unravel the symbolism by using the amplification and word association techniques.

6. Resting Time.   Allow a fallow period to let the issue go if an immediate answer fails to appear.

7. Further Examine the Responses.   Become alert to any additional flashes of insight.

8. Implement or Activate the Solution.   Implement the advice received from the intuitive mind.

ADDRESSING SPECIFIC HEALTH CONCERNS

Clarifying the Background and Issue

By stating your problem precisely, you will elicit imagery more readily and clearly. For example, instead of asking, "What's going on with my back?" you would ask, "What is the meaning of my chronic lower back problem?"

I showed you how to take the first step of defining your issue in Chapter 2. Remember to focus on one issue. For example, do not ask, "Should I go to a new doctor and get a prescription for a new supplement?" These are two separate inquiries, each inviting a separate reply. Make your focus very tight—one issue. Here are some examples: "What type of specialist should I see?" "Should I go to an herbalist?" "Is this the right salve for my bruised knee?"

In the following cases, notice how the background concerns are separated from the main inquiry. Also, notice the shifts in perspective the inner physician provides in helping these people reverse their health challenges.

MINDSHIFT METHOD: APPLICATION

Framing the Issue

Laurie.　　Laurie wanted to find out how to strengthen her brittle bones. The *background* of her problem is that she had unexpected surgery to remove a possibly cancerous tumor. Thankfully, the tumor was benign and easily removed. But during her long recovery period, Laurie became very thin and frail. As a result of the surgery, her body did not produce sufficient estrogen and her bones turned brittle. Not realizing this, the doctors concluded that Laurie had severe osteoporosis.

Puzzled and alarmed that this young lady of thirty-two had such a dangerous disease, the doctors ran many tests, seeking the cause of her weakened bones. Laurie found her condition especially hard to accept; she had always been very active, and now her doctors did not want her to exercise for very long. To frame her *issue*, Laurie asked, "Will my bones become strong and healthy again?"

Joan.   Joan wanted to have a child. She had been married for nine years, and for the last five she had tried unsuccessfully to conceive. She and her husband went to a fertility specialist who gave them several options. None of the options had 100 percent certainty, and Joan was concerned. For her issue, Joan asked, "Will I ever get pregnant?"

Stan.   Stan traveled to New York from California to help his sister through an illness. When he returned, Stan caught a cold for the first time in years. It settled into his head, nose, and chest and put him into bed for two or three days. At first he chalked the cold up to stress, travel, and the need to take a rest. But having learned the Mindshift Method, he decided to explore the message his body was giving through his illness. Stan framed his issue with the question "Why did I contract this cold after my trip?"

Centering and Receptivity

These two steps are complementary because first you are releasing the mental chatter and then you are clearing the tension from the body.

Laurie.   To begin her shift into her intuitive mind, Laurie imagined herself resting on a Florida beach. She became centered by watching the waves crashing on the shore. In this wonderful setting, she became receptive by taking several reenergizing breaths followed by the progressive relaxation technique.

Joan.   To begin her shift into her intuitive mind, Joan went downstairs to her treadmill and started running. Her eyes focused on the grain of the wall's wood paneling; listening to the whir of the treadmill's motor and the rhythmic pounding of her feet on the track, she fell into a reverie. Her breathing became measured. In her mind's eye, she pictured herself running through the forest on a path covered with leaves.

Stan.   To begin his shift into his intuitive mind, Stan gazed at a beautiful seashell on his desk and silently repeated the affirmation "My intuitive mind will lead me to the right answer." He also took several total breaths and consciously relaxed his body.

Eliciting and Interpreting the Imagery

Become alert to passive signals, such as flashes, or actively probe for an intuitive reply. You are fishing for an intuitive picture, symbol, image, or brief message. Notice how Laurie was *actively* involved in the imagery process. On the other hand, the imagery appeared *passively* for Joan and Stan after they became centered and receptive, and once again posed the issue to the intuitive mind.

Laurie.   Laurie, now relaxed on her inner beach, saw seashells being continually washed ashore. With eyes closed, she then actively elicited this imagery and imagined these shells forming a strong framework in her body. To interpret the seashell imagery, she used the amplification technique and came up with the following associations.

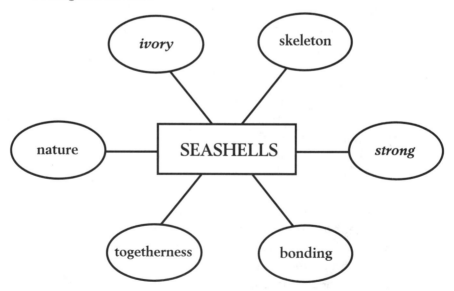

Laurie imagined the shells as strong, hard, skeletal pieces of material, washing onto the beach and bonding together, forming a substance of strength. Each shell was ivory in color, just like her bones. In this way she visualized her bones, like these shells, fusing together and growing strong and solid. She pictured her body in motion, like the sea. And she incorporated this feeling and imagery of flowing movement, of healing waves, into her body. Trusting this imagery, she felt a sense of peace and intuitively *knew* that her bones would heal and become strong again. She also knew that this renewed confidence itself would help her to heal. Laurie was one of my students when she applied the Mindshift Method to her health challenge. Three months later, she came into class smiling. The doctor had verified what her intuitive mind had known all along—her bones had become strong again.

Joan. The following images arose in Joan's mind's eye. First she felt warmth in her womb and saw an image of the sun coming up over the horizon. Then she saw a newborn baby in a bassinet and her husband reaching down to pick the child up. She saw herself standing at his side. They were both looking at the baby and smiling. Then she saw her mother's face, also smiling.

Joan now interpreted the first image using word association. She noticed that baby in the bassinet ⇒ bass ⇒ lower note ⇒ bottom ⇒ *new line coming in*. Feeling wonderful about the intuitive insight of a new line coming in, Joan closed her eyes and reconnected with the initial image of the sun coming up over the horizon. This was another confirmation of her son coming up in the near future.

Joan now intuitively felt that she would become pregnant and have a son. She now consciously visualized the sun rising in her womb and felt its healing warmth. She realized this powerful image was a healing gift from her inner physician, and felt certain that by working with it over time she would conceive. Her anxiety over this issue gave way to a sense of peace, a sign of the workings of intuition. Ten months later I received an announcement of the birth of her son, Alex, from Joan.

Stan. Stan associated the word "cold," for his illness, with a sense of chilliness and aloneness. This made him realize that although it had been very stressful being with his sister and brother-in-law at a time when her life was on the line, the possibility of losing her made their time together poignant and sweet. The three of them had talked in deep and loving ways about real things in a way they had never done before. Much emotion and love had been expressed and shared. In short, his visit there had warmed his heart. And he now saw, by comparison with this, the lack of such *warmth* in his day-to-day life. Nothing was bad or wrong, but he missed the genuine intimacy and love that he had experienced on his visit. And he felt the coldness of its absence.

Stan had been prepared to simply resume his old life. But now he saw that it was too cold for his taste, and he felt a desire to change this. Having seen what is possible in human relationships, Stan began reaching out to old friends in a new way, engaging them more deeply and enjoying their friendship. A longtime bachelor, he also decided it was time to allow a new love to come into his life. And all this came from allowing his inner physician to speak to him about the meaning of a common cold. And to think that he might have merely cured his cold with aspirin and a few days of rest!

You have just seen how three people used the Mindshift Method to become centered and receptive and then to elicit and interpret imagery that helped them resolve their health issues. Often the initial process is the first round, as further questions arise for consideration. In the association and interpretation phase of the Mindshift process, try not to become too analytical. Left-brained speculation and psychologizing is not the same as your inner physician's intuitive wisdom.

Now let's do one more Mindshift Method walk-through to view the process in its entirety.

Walking Through the Mindshift Method

Background. Al has taken a leave of absence from a company where he has worked for thirty years. Worn out, he harbors a secret desire to take a safari to Africa. He also feels beleaguered in his personal life: his ex-wife has run up major debts for which he is responsible. And he implores his friends, "Please, don't tell me anything she's doing. I don't want to hear it."

Strangely enough, he suffers a hearing loss that comes and goes. The doctors are unable to locate the cause of his malady. So Al decides to engage the Mindshift Method, hoping to discover both the cause for his hearing condition and a cure.

Issue.   Al asks, "What keeps me from hearing?"

Centering.   Al rises early, goes to his study, and sits at his desk. He gazes for several minutes at a multicolored rock he found on a family outing.

Receptivity.   He takes several hang-sah breaths, closes his eyes, and relaxes his body. Then he goes through the tense-and-release technique, which puts him in a receptive state.

Imagery.   Now Al asks his inner physician how he can regain his hearing. Two images appear to him. First he sees a stethoscope. Then he sees the Berlin Wall being broken down. This image is poignant for Al, who visited that historic site after the wall was torn down.

Interpret the Imagery.   Al considers the word "stethoscope"; many associations come forth: instrument, medical, amplify. Then an "Aha!" comes. A stethoscope is used to listen to the heart. Al realizes that he needs to listen to his heart, which has been telling him to make a clean break with his wife, instead of his head, which has been telling him to hang on and try to collect the money she owes him. Now he understands the Berlin Wall image—he needs to have an opening. In fact, he needs to be open to making a clean break with his ex-wife, whether she repays the debt or not. This is what he doesn't want to hear.

Resting Time.   Al takes a break from this initial flood of insight.

Further Examine the Responses.   Later he feels the need to continue this Mindshift process, and he asks, "What do I need for completion?" He sees an image of two people shaking hands. Could this be an agreement? Perhaps good-bye? Al isn't sure. He uses the image of a traffic light for clarification. Should his relationship with his wife continue or end? The red light goes on. This suggests that he stop the relationship without further agitation.

Implement.   Al makes his break in several steps. He takes time throughout the day to picture his ex-wife and affirm, "I release my hold on you and wish you well. Thank you for releasing your hold on me and wishing me well." Then he imagines them shaking hands and parting amicably. He resolves to pay his ex-wife's present debts, and he gets her agreement that he is not liable for any future debts. They part amicably. Al now feels freer, clearer, and hugely relieved. He is no longer worried about what he might hear about his ex-wife. And his hearing condition mysteriously disappears.

These four case stories show the varying causes and meanings underlying many health conditions. As we saw with Stan and Al, many physical ailments are connected to unresolved emotional conflicts and life situations. And as we saw with Laurie and Joan, even when a physical ailment doesn't clearly reflect a non-physical condition, the Mindshift Method can still elicit useful insights and imagery through which health can be restored.

Now it is time for you to try the Mindshift process.

PRACTICE: USING THE MINDSHIFT TO UNDERSTAND A HEALTH CHALLENGE

Choose a physical ailment to work with, whether a nagging pain in your neck or back, headache, upset stomach, and so on. If you are pain-free at this time, think of a friend or a family member who has a particular health problem. Chronicle the background surrounding the ailment and then succinctly state your issue.

Background _____

_____

_____

_____

_____

Issue _____

_____

_____

Become centered and release the mental tension by affirming, selecting a focusing word or two, or looking at a focusing object. What are you doing to become centered?

Centering _____

_____

_____

Record what breathing and relaxation techniques you used to become receptive. How did this help you shift from the logical to the intuitive mind?

Breathing _____

_____

_____

Relaxation _____

_____

_____

What imagery can your inner physician provide to help you find clarity? If you need to actively probe for an intuitive reply, create imagery such as a traffic stoplight or a lighted sign reading yes or no.

Imagery _____

_____

_____

Now to interpret this puzzling symbolism, use the amplification or word association techniques. Use this space to interpret and unravel the symbolism.

Interpretation _____

_____

_____

Do you need a resting time to incubate a response?

Resting time _____

_____

Have any other questions arisen? Have any additional insights surfaced since the question was initially posed?

Further interpretation _____

_____

_____

How are you going to implement the advice you received from the intuitive mind?

Implementation _____

_____

_____

Coping with Change

Transitions and change are necessary parts of life. In my seminars, workshops, and talks, I often ask at the outset if anyone is going through a transition. Inevitably, most of the audience raises their hands. As you read through the following cases, which deal with change, notice how the individuals using the Mindshift Method were able to transform agitation and discomfort into productive, healing solutions.

Lilia.   Lilia, who suffers from chronic respiratory problems, used the Mindshift Method to see if perhaps there was an underlying nonphysical cause to her condition. She feels trapped in an unhappy marriage. Communication in her marriage is almost nonexistent, and for the past year she has been working up the courage to tell her husband she wants a divorce. After becoming centered and relaxed, she posed the question "How can I get rid of my upper respiratory inflammation?"

Surprisingly, she saw the image of a phone with steam coming out of it. The phone, of course, is a vehicle for communication, and Lilia realized she must talk to her husband about her discontent. Reflecting back on the past year, she realized that every time she had wanted to broach the subject of divorce, she came down with a serious infection. Now she saw this was directly related to her failure to express her anger to husband. By not letting off steam through communication, she was making herself sick. Next she asked, "How can I communicate my anger and my need for a divorce?" The image of a Japanese rock garden surfaced. Fond of Japanese gardens, Lilia understood this to mean that she should make her communication simple and sparse, and keep a peaceful center.

Kris.   Kris, a human resources administrator in a hospital, used the Mindshift Method to cope with the stress created by the reorganization of her department—a circumstance affecting not only her but also her staff of seven employees. Hoping to provide a positive work environment for herself and her staff and to cut down on the collective stress, Kris asked, "How can I relieve the frustration and reduce the stress levels of my employees?" She saw the image of two old women moving up and down on a teeter-totter.

The associations that came to her for this image included the words "play" and "balance." With this "Aha!" she saw that she and her staff needed to play in order to achieve balance in their stressed-out work environment. As Christmas was rapidly approaching, Kris arranged to have an office Christmas party, full of fun and games. This party did in fact break the tension that had plagued the staff for months, and set a new and more playful mood in the office.

PRACTICE: COPING WITH CHANGE

With this practice we'll examine how you are currently coping with any transition or difficult change in your life. Write down any changes you are presently experiencing. _____

_____

_____

Frame your issue with a clear question, take the Mindshift steps of centering and becoming receptive, then elicit and interpret intuitive imagery. Record your results. _____

_____

_____

_____

Now let's see how you are coping with these changes. Close your eyes and imagine a vertical scale or thermometer with the numbers one through ten running from the bottom to the top. Ask, "How am I coping with this change?" and watch to see where the mercury stops. You can also simply think of the numbers one through ten and see if a number effortlessly appears in your mind in response to this question.

How did you rate yourself? _____

_____

Would you like to improve your rating? If so, request an image that symbolizes what you can do to improve your coping skills. Record your insights. _____

_____

_____

_____

A DOCTOR'S INVOLVEMENT

If a genie could grant me one wish, it would be that all the people actively engaged in the healing professions would acknowledge and use their own intuition in their practice. This means doctors, nurses, health-care workers, educators, psychotherapists, bodyworkers, human service and mental health practitioners, gerontologists, and so forth. To some degree, this is beginning to happen. I've met many physicians and nurses around the country who admit to using their intuition when diagnosing and treating patients. These practitioners are pioneers in what will be the future paradigm of the healing profession.

One such pioneer is Dr. Lawrence Burk, Jr., a professor of radiology at the Duke University Medical Center in Durham, North Carolina. Dr. Burk read my *Intuition Workbook*, which he used to hone his intuitive skills. While using the "house of intuition" exercise, he had a breakthrough. This practice is an exercise in intuitive problem solving in which one finds a message in an imaginary book or an object in an imaginary box that gives a solution to a dilemma. Dr. Burk found that this exercise in simple imagery provided him with valuable intuitive insights for his medical practice and enabled him to tap into the subconscious, not only of individual patients, but also of humanity as a whole—what Carl Jung terms the collective unconscious.

Dr. Burk was introduced to anodyne imagery—a body/mind technique for helping patients cope with pain and anxiety during stressful procedures—via a series of weekend workshops in his radiology department. Now he wanted the hospital administration to sponsor a similar training program for the other departments. Fortunately, another physician on the staff was equally enthusiastic. Having seen what Dr. Burk had done in the radiology department, this specialist in pulmonary medicine saw how the technique of anodyne imagery might be used to perform bronchoscopies without sedation. This physician discussed funding for such training with the chief administrator. But several weeks went by with no news.

Dr. Burk then used the Mindshift Method, hoping to find a way to get funding. After entering the receptive state, he affirmed that his intuitive mind would lead him to a positive resolution and asked, "How can I get the hospital administration to sponsor a similar training program for other departments?"

Next, using the "house of intuition" imagery, Dr. Burk went in his imagination to his favorite natural setting—a garden. Then the image of a house appeared, and he entered the front door. Once inside, he ascended a staircase to a library filled with bookshelves. He scanned the shelves randomly, expecting to find the answer to his question in one of the books. Finally he selected a book, opened it, and read the phrase "build something." When no immediate associations came with this phrase, he decided the answer would likely be found in a box next to the bookshelf. He opened the box and unexpectedly found a gun, a somewhat startling image. However, his free association with this image elicited the words "bullets" and then "magic bullets." He did not quite know what to make of this.

The next day he visited the pulmonologist to find out what was happening with the funding proposal. To his surprise, the pulmonologist told him, "I just saw the chief administrator. He said that he respected my input and that I can have one favor a year from him. And he said if this proposal is how I want to spend my silver bullet, then it's okay with him." The pulmonologist then told Dr. Burk that he was "going to fire that magic bullet right now." The proposal was subsequently approved. The puzzling imagery of the day before now became clear to Dr. Burk. His intuition was telling him that the situation was already resolved. He could now begin to help "build" the new training programs.

Dr. Burk has since found the "house of intuition" to be a useful technique for intuitive problem solving in many areas.

Chapter Six

THE PROACTIVE POSTURE
FOR MAINTAINING PERFECT
HEALTH

PROACTIVE LIVING IS THE BEST MEDICINE

An ounce of prevention is worth a pound of cure," my grandmother loved to say. "Proactive" is the modern word for such preventive measures. But modern medicine is almost exclusively reactive, not a cultivation of health, but a belated response to health already lost. Bad habits set us on a collision course with exhaustion, disease, and premature aging. Yet radiant health can be had with just a little effort by anyone. This chapter concerns simple, powerful proactive or preventive health strategies that can be incorporated into the busiest life. These energizing, life-enhancing practices call on the skills you have been cultivating through the Mindshift Method exercises in this book—centering, relaxation, breathing, imagination, and imagery retrieval. These are the key ingredients for accessing your intuitive mind and communicating with your inner physician.

Today we can be healthier and stronger and live longer than any generation before us. This is due to the dramatic increase in knowledge about diet and nutrition, the general availability of quality food and cutting-edge nutritional supplements, the proliferation of health clubs, and general awareness of the hazards of high cholesterol and substance abuse.

Today in our culture, fitness, or radiant health, is an idea whose time has come. And such health can be had, with the expenditure of a little effort on a regular basis. Yet the pressures of our daily lives can easily sabotage our resolve and lead to bad health habits. Often our good intentions dissolve when we arrive at work, a pressured and stressful environment. Many employees are overworked and underpaid, fearful of not making ends meet or of being fired or eliminated through downsizing. In such an environment, good health intentions often fall by the wayside.

However, an individual working with the intuitive mind has a most powerful ally and is not at a loss. His or her inner physician is available at a moment's notice, even in the most stressful situation, to offer wise counsel.

Research has shown that people who are burned out can't tell the difference between intuition, fear, and wishful thinking—their circuits are jammed. Certain simple practices are the key to proactive stress management and the source of radiant health.

Quantum physicians like Dr. Deepak Chopra tell us that our mind actually exists in every cell of our bodies and that our thoughts and feelings can alter our bodily chemistry. The road to Wellville begins in the mind, under the guidance of your inner physician. Now let us examine the simple steps contained in the Mindshift Method. The key points we will be working with are receptivity (breathing and relaxation), centering, and imagery retrieval—three powerful proactive tools for achieving and maintaining optimum health.

RECEPTIVITY: BREATHING

We all know the basics of good health: eat right and get plenty of exercise and rest. But there are other equally important proactive steps we can take to achieve radiant health. Remember, man does not live by bread alone. What substance do we require even more urgently than food and drink? Oxygen, of course—the breath of life.

Poor breathing habits cause untold misery, depleting the vital energy, dulling the mind, and toxifying the blood. In one day, the heart pumps 35,000 pints of blood through the body. The blood passing through our system absorbs toxins, which are meant to be strained out by our lungs and oxygenated by our breath. But as most of us tend to take shallow breaths, blood and brain are underoxygenated, and the toxins are recirculated through the body until they are purified through nature's last resort—illness. Then the cycle begins again.

The simple solution is deep breathing. When we inhale deeply through the nose as we are meant to do, remarkable things happen. Deep breathing through the nostrils directly stimulates the brain, making us alert, upbeat, and energetic. (Practitioners of yoga claim that proper breathing over time awakens higher brain functioning and psychic abilities.)

But without sufficient oxygen, proper digestion and elimination cannot occur; we do not absorb enough nutrients from our food, a major cause of overeating. Poor digestion and elimination flood the body with toxins that come from food literally rotting in the belly.

Proper breathing boosts the immune system, both directly and indirectly, by taking more energy into our systems, and also by stimulating our internal organs to more efficient functioning. One deep breath, expanding the tummy and lungs to full capacity, works bona fide wonders for health. When the lungs expand to full capacity, the innumerable spongy sacs where toxins often accumulate, resulting in respiratory illnesses such as chest colds and bronchitis, are cleansed.

The tummy, expanded by full breathing, receives the oxygen it needs to properly digest and eliminate the food. This means maximum nutrition, minimum toxicity, and therefore increased energy from the food we eat—which means we will be likely to eat less. Also, the tummy and lungs, expanded by such deep breathing, press against and massage the internal organs—liver, kidneys, intestines, and heart—stimulating and improving their functioning. Five minutes a day of proper breathing is more beneficial to the human body than the most nutritious meal. No vitamin can deliver the health benefits of such breathing. This simple procedure can be learned with a little practice.

Complete breathing also puts you in a natural meditative or intuitive state and immediately increases your ability to concentrate and absorb information. This is why I suggest breathing and relaxation as one of the initial stages of the Mindshift Method.

EXERCISE: PROPER BREATHING—THE TOTAL BREATH

Sit erect in a chair with your hands in your lap. Now breathe slowly through the nostrils into the belly. When the belly is full, continue inhaling into the solar plexus. When the solar plexus is full, continue inhaling until the chest is fully expanded. This is a complete inhale, done in a smooth and gradual expansion. Now, hold the breath in for a count of eight, then exhale slowly in reverse. Let the air out of the chest, then out of the solar plexus; last, force all the air out of the belly with some muscular effort. This is the total breath, or the belly breath.

Repeat the total breath described above ten times, and then sit quietly for a minute with your eyes closed. Notice the difference in how you feel. If your mind is dull or you feel groggy, after ten complete breaths you will feel alert and energetic, yet deeply relaxed.

Describe how you feel. _____

_____

_____

If you practice this total breath for five minutes a day, you will receive all the health benefits mentioned. It is a marvelous way to wake yourself up and begin your day. When you are feeling groggy at work, at school, or at any time, you can change your state in moments with a few total breaths. Proper breathing is a simple, effective health strategy. Make room in your daily life for deep breathing and you will be truly astonished by the results.

RECEPTIVITY: RELAXATION

Relaxation is the next proactive health strategy, the other component of the receptivity step in the Mindshift Method. We all know it is good to relax, but many of us never learn how. The ability to relax is a skill that must be learned like any other. The tense-and-release relaxation technique is given in Chapter 2 (page 32). But first, why is relaxation so important?

Because relaxation releases stress, which causes tension, anxiety, fatigue, toxicity, and a weakened immune system—the perfect recipe for every kind of poor health. When the body is tense, toxins are locked into tissues and muscles. Bodyworkers tell us that old trauma and emotional pain are also stored in our body as tension. When our body relaxes, the toxins and stresses stored there are released, and we can experience a natural state of well-being. Relaxation thus helps purify the body of toxins, release stress, and balance the emotions. Conscious relaxation also lowers blood pressure and reduces the likelihood of hypertension, heart trouble, insomnia, and nervous disorders. But there is another interesting benefit of relaxation.

I've seen accounts of research that have shown that if we get into bed and simply fall asleep, the body needs three to five hours to relax to the point where it can begin what is known as rejuvenating sleep. The body must release enough of the accumulated tensions of the day before this most beneficial period of sleep can occur. But if we consciously relax the body for five to ten minutes before falling asleep, we can then fall directly into rejuvenating sleep. In other words, through conscious relaxation, we can release in five to ten minutes the tension it takes the body three to five hours to release during regular sleep. This means that we will get from three to five hours more rejuvenating sleep, will probably sleep less, and will wake up more refreshed.

Conscious relaxation thus reverses the cycle of tension, enervation, and illness that so many of us go through. Five to ten minutes a day of conscious relaxation can mean a world of difference to health. The following relaxation practice is designed to be undergone at night before falling asleep, or at any time of the day when you need to recharge your energy or release any stress you might be feeling.

PRACTICE: CONSCIOUS RELAXATION

Lie on your back on the bed (or floor), your arms at your side. Take several deep breaths. Relax your body, using the tense-and-release method, starting with the feet and working all the way up to the head. You can tense and relax everything by twos (feet, calves, knees, thighs, and so on). When you finish this, feel your entire body to be relaxed and heavy, a field of energized matter, which is what you are. Enjoy being truly relaxed.

Now, see yourself at the top of a flight of stairs or an escalator, going down, down, down. Tell yourself that you are growing more relaxed as you descend. If you have difficulty visualizing this, simply count backward from ten or twenty to zero and remind yourself that you are growing more relaxed with each count. As you do this, enjoy the feeling of relaxing more and more deeply.

After you have taken ten to twenty steps down (as needed), or counted down to zero, you should be in a state of deep relaxation. You can maintain this state by simply feeling this relaxation, keeping your mind in your body, and anchoring your attention on your breath as it goes in and out. If you are afraid you might simply fall asleep, bend your right arm so that your elbow is resting on the mattress (or floor) and your hand is pointing at the ceiling. Exert only enough tension to keep the arm in this position. Now if you start to fall asleep, the arm will begin to fall, bringing you back into deep-relaxation consciousness. Remain in this state as an observer and notice what you see, feel, or experience.

In this relaxed or intuitive state, you may experience spontaneous hypnogogic imagery, semi-waking dreams, unusual insights, and pleasant sensations of heaviness, fullness, or flowing energy. This state can also be used for problem-solving and positive self-programming. If you ask for solutions and creative ideas in this state, they will often come when you need them. But the very least you can expect from this simple practice are the health benefits of the relaxation itself.

When you are ready to return to your normal waking state, count slowly from one to ten, telling yourself that you will awaken feeling refreshed, energized, alert, and happy.

Record your experience. _____

_____

_____

ALTERNATIVE PRACTICE: THE AUTOGENIC RELAXATION METHOD

This autogenic relaxation technique is an equally effective method for achieving a state of deep relaxation.

Use the hang-sah breath you learned in Chapter 2 (page 31) to enter the alpha level. Slowly inhale whispering "hang" and slowly exhale while whispering "sah." Listen to the hypnotic sound of your own whispered breath. Do this nine times.

Silently or aloud send these messages to each part of your body.

My feet feel warm and relaxed. My feet feel warm and relaxed. My feet are warm and relaxed.

My legs feel warm and relaxed. My legs feel warm and relaxed. My legs are warm and relaxed.

My midsection feels warm and relaxed. My midsection feels warm and relaxed. My midsection is warm and relaxed.

My chest and back feel warm and relaxed. My chest and back feel warm and relaxed. My chest and back are warm and relaxed.

My arms feel warm and relaxed. My arms feel warm and relaxed. My arms are warm and relaxed.

My shoulders and neck feel warm and relaxed. My shoulders and neck feel warm and relaxed. My shoulders and neck are warm and relaxed.

My face and head feel warm and relaxed. My face and head feel warm and relaxed. My face and head are warm and relaxed.

Affirm
Every cell in my body feels relaxed and comfortable.
Every cell in my body feels relaxed and comfortable.
Every cell in my body is relaxed and comfortable.
I am now totally relaxed.

To reenter your normal state of consciousness, use the same method of counting from one to ten, programming yourself to awaken refreshed, energized, alert, and happy. Record your experience below.

_____
_____
_____
_____
_____
_____

Remember, doing ten minutes of conscious or autogenic relaxation is worth hours of sleep. And the skill gained through this simple practice will creep into every aspect of your daily life. Soon the relaxed state can be accessed by simply deciding to relax, for the neural pathways have been formed. Then practice random moments of relaxation throughout the day; thirty seconds sitting at your desk or in a parked car restores your energy and returns you to your center. Increasingly, you will feel calmer under pressure, function more efficiently in the face of stress, and know how to release tension whenever it arises. This is key to the maintenance of radiant health.

CENTERING

The skill of relaxation can be combined with another powerful health technique—centering. In the Mindshift Method, centering is the use of a phrase, affirmation, prayer, or visualization that helps us let go and bring ourselves into our center, the calm eye of our own spirit in the apparent storm of our often hectic lives.

In his extraordinary book *Ageless Body, Timeless Mind*, Deepak Chopra informs us that researchers have discovered that our every thought instantaneously changes our bodily chemistry. Disturbed and chaotic thoughts and emotions not only remove us from our center but send destructive chemicals racing through our bloodstream. Ulcers are only the most obvious example of the havoc wrought on the body in this way.

The practice of centering allows us to release destructive patterns of thought and emotion and return to the peace of our center, or spirit, experiencing its natural healing power. In Chapter 2, I suggested several centering affirmations, such as "The divine energy flowing through every cell of my body creates radiant health." Visualizing this image while repeating this phrase has a profoundly healing and balancing effect on the body, mind, and emotions. You can also use more religious affirmations, such as "I am in the hands of the Goddess" or "the light of Spirit now illumines my being."

Such powerful affirmations or prayers used while visualizing light brightening the body and mind or feeling the sense of a divine presence have extraordinary healing power. These powerful practices, which can produce radiant health, are the same ancient methods used in every religion to contact the divine power or inner self to achieve spiritual transformation.

Color Healing

You can use other centering techniques in conjunction with the practice of conscious relaxation. Color meditation is another powerful healing technique. In this meditation, you access the healing or energies of various colors by visualizing them filling and surrounding your body. Here are some commonly accepted interpretations of the energy qualities of various colors cited in books on color therapy.

Red Energy and action: recharging and energizing; physical, sexual energy; anger; fear; anxiety

Orange Balance: symmetry between mind and emotions; harmony; consideration

Yellow The mind: logical thinking; investigation; communication; joy

Green Emotion: love; growth; life energy; healing; prosperity

Light Blue Introspective: conceptual; deeper knowledge; inner peace

Indigo Intuitive: sixth sense; insight; vision; clear understanding

Violet Transformation: spiritual; imagination; fantasy; higher mind; divine order

So try them out and see how they feel to you.

PRACTICE: COLOR HEALING

Go to any part of your body that is ailing. Focus on that area and ask your intuitive mind to send you a message in the form of a color about that area. For example, Ruth, a singer, focused on her throat and got the color indigo. This is clearly telling her that she has to trust her intuition about her throat. She has to listen to her inner physician, who has been prescribing ginger tea to help soothe the raspiness in her throat.

Go into *your* ailing area to retrieve a color that is transmitting information about your healing connection. Describe the color as well as your interpretation of this intuitive input. _____

_____

_____

_____

_____

_____

Call upon the other color for proactive healing when you need to bring a particular quality or essence into your life. For example, when you need to feel more balance in your life, garb yourself in orange. Try wearing red when you want more energy. Use green to heal any area of your body that is ailing. Imagine your inner physician painting that area green.

Record your experiences with color healing. _____

_____

_____

_____

_____

IMAGERY RETRIEVAL

Another powerful method for positive health programming is internal imaging. Visualizing yourself running freely, dancing wildly, swimming powerfully in a state of radiant health infuses the body with healing chemistry. Such active visualization programs an internal self-image of dynamic health that will likely prove prophetic. This technique is currently used by body builders to help them sculpt the perfect physique, just as professional athletes use it to hone their physical skills.

The Physical Benefits of Imaginary Exercise

The results of an amazing study[1] conducted at a Canadian hospital showed that imaginary exercise results in surprising health benefits. In the study, one group of cardiac patients performed physical exercise, while a second group exercised only in their imaginations.

Remarkably, this second group recovered their health more quickly than the group actually exercising. The following exercise, which I used in my *Intuition Workbook*, applies this knowledge, with a little color therapy added.

PRACTICE: TAKING AN IMAGINARY JOG

Do the following practice once a day for two minutes.

Go to your Mindshift area, where you will not be disturbed. Close your eyes, take three deep breaths, and see yourself putting on a red jogging suit and red sneakers. (If you like, you can even wear a red cape!) See yourself going out of your home and walking to the park. Enter the park and start running clockwise laps. Notice any tingling sensations in your body—this is the life energy stimulated through the kinesthetic response. Be aware of everything you see. (Is your red cape flying out behind you?) Be aware of what you sense and feel, of the wind on your face, the smell and spongy feel of the grass beneath your feet. Feel your stride and your breathing. Notice the trees, the sky. Complete your run at the point where you started. Then walk out of the park, back home. Take off your red jogging clothes, shower, dry off, and put on the clothes you are going to wear for the day.

Then open your eyes. How do you feel? If you prefer swimming, cycling, or in-line dancing, feel free to substitute them for jogging.

Do this for one week and record any changes you notice. _____

_____

_____

_____

Imagine This: From the Beginning to the End

Here is another way you can use visualization to program positive new health habits and achieve desired health goals. I call this method the alpha-to-omega technique. In this technique, visualize the current status of an issue (the beginning, or alpha), and continue creating the imagery that will take you to the desired ending (omega). Here is how Kristi used the alpha-to-omega technique to shed unwanted pounds.

First, she saw herself in her present overweight condition and felt her determination to lose weight. Next she pictured herself beginning her new diet and enjoying the taste of her new meals. She visualized herself at the grocery store, buying only healthy foods—fresh fruits and vegetables, yogurt, fish, potatoes, and high-fiber cereals. She visualized her daily exercise routine of walking ten brisk laps around a nearby soccer field. And in her mind's eye, she stood on a scale and watched the numbers going down, slowly but surely. She saw herself fitting into old clothes she had not been able to wear in years. And she saw herself in the end, slim, trim, and fit as a fiddle, jogging triumphantly around the soccer field.

Then she pictured a calendar and turned the pages of the months, starting with January and intuitively stopping at May. This is the time she will allot herself to reach her desired new weight, twenty pounds less than she weighs now. Kristi resolved to view this alpha-to-omega internal imagery script on a weekly basis, every Sunday afternoon, until the weight is gone.

PRACTICE: DEVISING YOUR OWN ALPHA-TO-OMEGA SCRIPT

Now modify Kristi's script to envision your own future healthy self. If your weight is not a problem, choose another issue that has relevance to you. Be creative and have fun with this. Enjoy the process of making new changes, and anticipate with pleasure the new you that you will soon be in reality. _____

_____

_____

_____

INTENTIONS, BELIEFS, AND HIDDEN ISSUES

To achieve and maintain a state of radiant health requires determination. Yet sometimes, though we desire such health, we fail to incorporate into our lives the simple principles that would turn this desire into a reality. I can give three reasons for this phenomenon. One is that we view the cultivation of health in a negative light—as drudgery and self-denial. Thus, the admonition to focus on the pleasures of exercise, a healthy diet, and so on. A second reason our good intentions may falter is due to hidden, self-sabotaging beliefs we may have about ourselves. Here is one example of how our beliefs can affect our health. For years my husband, Jim, got a cold every spring. Then one day he remembered his mother telling him as a child that getting a cold every spring was "good spring cleaning." When he made this connection—his cold was created by the belief that he would get a cold in the spring—his colds stopped.

A person wishing to lose weight may believe that because his mother and grandmother were heavy, overweight is just in his genes; nothing he can do will change it. You can see how such a belief might thwart the best of intentions. Or an out-of-shape person who wishes to begin a weight-lifting regimen or go running three times a week may unconsciously think: "My father had his heart attack while he was playing tennis. All that straining and sweating and pounding can't be good for my heart and body." Or, "I'm just not a disciplined person. I never keep things like that up." Again, you can see how negative beliefs work against our good intentions.

Third, hidden issues can often underlie our dilemmas over such things as weight problems, physical exercise, and substance abuse. Janet had a chronic weight problem for years. No matter how hard she tried, she couldn't seem to shed those pounds. Then she began to explore her relationship to food, tracing it back to her childhood. And she realized that her mother, a repressed, emotionally inexpressive woman, had expressed her love for her only by giving her food. Ever since, Janet had related to food as if it were her mother's love. But no amount of food could ever satisfy her craving for her mother's love. After receiving this insight, Janet was able to let go of the unconscious equation: food = mother's love. She lost twenty-five pounds, which she has kept off to this day.

Such issues underlie many of our unhealthy habits and sabotage our good intentions. Using the Mindshift Method, enlist the help of your inner physician, your intuitive mind, to uncover any minefields underlying your own struggle with particular health dilemmas. Then apply the alpha-to-omega practice given earlier, and success will certainly follow.

What hidden belief about your health would you like to expose? Become centered and receptive, and use any technique that enables you to meet your inner physician for a consultation. What belief would you like to explore? Your inner physician gives you a gift to help you understand what underlies this belief. This can come in the form of a picture that needs to be unwrapped, an article in a gift box, or an object handed to you.

What gift did you receive? _____

_____

Use amplification or word association to unravel the meaning of this gift.

How do you feel about receiving this gift? _____

_____

_____

How is awareness of what this symbolism means helping you eradicate this old belief? _____

_____

EAT, DRINK, EXERCISE, RELAX, AND BE MERRY, FOR TOMORROW WE LIVE

A few final words on the health measures we've all heard about since childhood: "Eat right, drink lots of fluids, and get plenty of exercise and rest." We are saturated with information on proper diet. But we hear little about a national epidemic of dehydration. Snapple, soda, coffee, and tea do not qualify as fluids in the health sense. Those fluids require water in order to be flushed out of our systems. Dehydration contributes to everything from general toxicity, dizziness, blackouts, and physical and mental torpor to kidney failure, heart attacks, and even premature aging, senility, and death. So the next time you feel that dryness in your mouth called thirst, have a glass of water on me. And make it a daily health habit.

As for rest, we are a nation suffering from chronic sleep deprivation. So if you can't get the rest you need, remedy this by practicing the relaxation methods given in this chapter. Once again, remember that ten minutes of conscious relaxation is worth several hours of sleep. By hook or by crook, you can get the rest you need.

I remember reading a study concluding that if one had a choice of either eating a terrible diet and exercising or of eating the perfect diet and not exercising, you would be healthier choosing the terrible diet with the exercise. Exercise is perhaps the most powerful proactive health strategy there is. Studies show that walking for fifteen minutes three times a week is enough to keep you in good physical condition. So do yourself a favor and take a hike.

And last, remember to pursue good health in right relationship to yourself and your own body. The cultivation of health should not feel like a war with yourself. If you think you are too fat, too thin, too short, too tall, too weak, or too strong, stop to remember and feel how lucky you are to simply be alive. Feel the simple pleasure of being alive. And remember to enjoy the gift.

This last exercise is called love, praise, and gratitude. Say it and feel it until you can mean it.

> *I love my body for the wonder it is.*
> *I may not be perfect,*
> *but I am divinely alive.*
> *I'm grateful for the health I have,*
> *And for this opportunity I've been given,*
> *To live in this incredible world.*
> *I praise the Marvelous Intelligence who made me,*
> *and the marvelous being I am becoming*
> *in my visions and in reality*
> *by the power of my spirit.*

Here's to your health!

Chapter Seven

HEARING THE INTUITIVE
BODY SPEAK

T he central theme of this book is that our words, thoughts, and feelings are vibrantly alive and have an impact on our bodies. Remember how a literal pain in the neck can be triggered by frustration and aggravation at a person who is a metaphorical pain in the neck? Or how a group of senior citizens remained healthy and active because they always believed they would? All your thoughts and memories, joys and sorrows, shocks and injuries, pleasures and pains, are stored in your muscles, tissues, and bones. Everything you've ever experienced or understood is literally embodied in you. This is the nature of the body/mind connection. We are infinitely complex, multidimensional beings with vast amounts of data genetically encoded in our very cells. Wow! And you thought it was just a body. Remarkably, you can communicate with your body, each part, and discover what issues, grievances, and pain reside in it, and heal it.

Whenever you feel stressed, out of sorts, or simply ill, you can access your inner physician as a trusted adviser, and in partnership with the miraculous intelligence in your cells, root up old memories presently inhabiting your body in the form of a pain in your arm, an ailing hip, a migraine headache, or a heart condition. This process will teach you how to release emotional pain long trapped in the body that has produced a physical malady. The result is holistic healing.

Putting an Ear to the Stethoscope

Two images exemplify the contents of this chapter: a stethoscope and an ear. The stethoscope is used by a doctor to amplify the internal activities of the body. In the same way your inner stethoscope—your *intuition*—amplifies what is occurring in your body/ mind. This stethoscope allows you to do a *body scan* to diagnose ailing areas and discover what needs to be realigned for healing to occur.

The second image, the ear, symbolizes receptivity and comprehension. Both images are embodied in the work of Ilana Rubenfeld, an internationally known pioneer in the field of body/mind connections and the creator of the Rubenfeld Synergy Method, which integrates mind, body, emotions, and spirit. Ilana teaches her students, prospective bodyworkers, how to develop "listening" hands that receive information through touch—an ability you too will acquire as you learn to *listen* to your body in a new way.

The Body Speaks

The intelligence present in every cell of your body communicates in innumerable ways. A friend dreamed he was in a burning house and couldn't get his girlfriend out. He could not decipher the underlying message of this puzzling dream. Was it a warning to check his home for fire hazards? In dreams, the body is often symbolized as a house. And since fire is heat, the dream might have been warning of a fever or infection. But it might also have been telling him that he was involved in a risky situation with someone in trouble who was burning him up and whom he could not save. When I asked him about this last possibility, his eyes widened in the familiar "Aha!" look. He confirmed that he was constantly angered and frustrated by his troubled and troublesome girlfriend.

Creating a Metaphor

You can penetrate a person's character and learn the real story, what makes them tick, by using the metaphor technique given in my *Intuition Workbook*. Choose any person, study them intuitively, and create an image that seems to fit them. By comparing the person to something else—a movie or book title or character or an animal, for example—you can retrieve amazing insights about him or her.

For example, if I see you as an eagle, what does that suggest? Once I get the image, I need to amplify. My associations are that you might be independent and sharp-eyed and love freedom. But the real "Aha!" comes when I realize that you have *keen insight*, a clear, sharp view of any situation. You can also use this same method to enter your body and discover the issues underlying your physical ailments.

Your intuitive imagination allows you to enter any bodily part, engage it in a dialogue, and derive from it an image or metaphor that shows you how to remedy the situation. Remember Janis and her throbbing right knee in Chapter 3? Using this method to view her knee, she saw sagging rubber bands, and she used imagery to make them more taut. When she looked into this area for a color, she saw a light blue that reminded her of the igloos pictured in ice advertisements. She realized she needed to keep her knee cool and avoid excess heat in the shower or hot tub. When she listened to her knee for a song, she heard the golden oldie "You'll Never Walk Alone." At first Janis wondered if that meant she would need crutches or a cane. But her intuition told her that her knee alone was not the problem; her whole body needed treatment. She then realized that if she lost weight, it would help alleviate her knee problem.

People attending my healing seminars have gained tremendous insights into their health challenges using this technique. Jenny came down with diabetes a month after she turned fifty-three. She saw a pincushion stuck with needles; the color was red; and heard the song "If I Had a Hammer." She of course was the pincushion, constantly sticking herself with insulin needles. Red showed her anger. Jenny had been angry at family members, especially toward her brother, for years. She now saw how it had poisoned her life and affected her health, and knew she needed to "hammer it out" rather than continue to nurse her resentment, which was like sticking herself with pins.

Remember the commitment to healing you made in Chapter 3? Turn back to page 56 to see what you wanted to heal. Has there been any change in this condition? Does any other condition need to be added? Choose one health concern from your original list or any condition that has surfaced since that time. Now let's use your intuitive stethoscope to diagnose a physical ailment.

PRACTICE: SCOPING IT OUT

The body area I want to work on is _____

_____

_____

_____

_____

For this practice, you might want to put the directions on a cassette tape or have someone read them to you. If that is not possible, read the questions several times first, so you can recall them when you are settled into your quiet space.

Find a time and place where you will be undisturbed for fifteen minutes. Get in a comfortable position. Close your eyes and take three deep breaths. Really feel the air coming in and going out. Relax your body. Notice any distracting thoughts or feelings and let them go. If they persist, tell them that you will attend to them later but don't want to be disturbed right now. Now let images bubble up in your imagination. Observe them without interpreting them in any way. If no images arise, that is all right. Simply continue to relax and look within.

When you feel centered, use your imagination to walk right into this ailing bodily area. As you enter into it, what object, idea, or image comes to you?

Does this area remind you of a place?

If this area were a color, what color would it be?

Does a book, movie, or song title come to mind?

Does this area remind you of anyone you know personally? Of a famous person or a character in a book?

Can you come up with an image that seems to fit the pain?

What image can help you release the pain? For example, if you have sharp back pains, has someone stabbed you in the back? Then pull the knife out and let the wound heal.

As you prepare to return to outer awareness, silently count to five. One, two . . . three, move your fingers around . . . four, move your head from side to side . . . and five, slowly open your eyes and stretch. Record your images, metaphors, and insight. Take as much time as you need to amplify or interpret the material you gathered in this process. Write it down.

What *objects, ideas, or images* did you discover? _____

_____

_____

What do these things tell you about this area? _____

_____

If this area were a *color*, what color would it be? _____

_____

What associations do you make with this color? _____

_____

_____

_____

What *movie, book, or song title* came to you from this area? ____

_____

_____

How does the book or song title apply to this area? _____

_____

_____

_____

What *person or character*, intimate, famous, or fictional, is associated with this area? _____

_____

How or why do they remind you of this area? _____

_____

_____

As you integrate all the images and information you have received, what is your inner physician telling you about this ailing bodily part and how to heal it? _____

_____

_____
_____

BODY LANGUAGE

We have all heard how important body language is in our communication with others. Yet our bodies are always speaking to us, and we are often so busy, they find it hard to get our attention.

If you feel restless and out of sorts, your body may be telling you that you need a change of scenery. Those inner rumblings of discontent may indicate you should find solace in meditation, prayer, or a nature retreat. If you feel tired or depleted, your body is telling you to rest. And if you continually ignore its messages, you will be forced to rest by illness or injuries.

I always encourage my students to engage in a dialogue with their ailing bodily parts. In this way, they can heal their maladies with the help of their inner physicians, rather than just taking medication. Remember how Stan's cold led him to make changes in his life instead of simply taking aspirin?

In the case of Janis and her throbbing right knee, she asked her knee how it was feeling and what was needed for healing to take place. She sat with a pad and started writing down what she heard. Since Janis has been connecting to her intuitive mind for several years, her dialogue is very complete. If you are a novice, your dialogue might initially be rougher, with only snatches of ideas. What you elicit will smooth out eventually.

Here is a record from her journal of a dialogue she had with her knee over a four-day period.

First Day: You are really bent out of shape. Because you are emotionally bent out of shape, your body is also out of alignment. You need to get straightened out emotionally. Then you will feel good and confident. You need to bend to the changing tide of circumstances. Be more flexible.

Second Day: You are out of joint and out of phase. Start exercising me gently. When you are ready to go out and go forward, I will be, too. I am not only out of joint and bent out of shape, but you have been putting too much weight on me.

Third Day: If you take a load off your feet, you won't be burdening me so much. Prepare for the future as we dash forward. There is much to do and this time period has been set aside for you to collect and assimilate what you need for your future work. You will heal, but you need to make a commitment to have the excess weight come off.

Fourth Day: You are not bending to the circumstances in your life. The recent move to California was weighty, and many adjustments still have to be made in your new environment. As you bend and adjust, so will I. By the way, did anyone ever mention that you need a good rest? So when I send an ache to you in the knee, that means you need to get off your feet.

Now it is *your* turn to talk with any bodily part that is crying out for attention. See what you can find out. Have a dialogue with as many areas as you want. But keep a separate account for each part to avoid confusion. Later you can compare these accounts to see if there are any parallels, hidden connections, or overlapping themes. This is a wonderful way to get a metadiagnosis from your inner physician.

PRACTICE: HAVE A DIALOGUE WITH YOUR ACHING BODILY PART

For this practice, pick one area from your healing list. After you have received some insight about what this body part is trying to tell you, repeat the practice with another bodily part.

The bodily part I am having a dialogue with is _____

Day One _____

_____

_____

_____

Day Two _____

_____

_____

_____

Day Three _____

_____

_____

_____

Day Four _____

_____

_____

_____

On a separate piece of paper, keep a running record of your insights. Then put all the pieces of this body puzzle together. What common themes surface? _____

_____

_____

_____

What intuitive communication are you receiving from your inner physician about your body? _____

_____

_____

_____

TAKING A BODY X RAY

One weekend I sat in a seminar facilitated by Caroline Myss and was in awe of her ability to make highly accurate medical diagnoses of people she had never met. One female participant asked about a current health challenge. That was as much information as she gave. Caroline in turn asked only for the woman's name and age. Almost instantly, she told the woman where her physical problem *really* was, and more important, she identified which factors and circumstances in her life created this condition.

Dr. Myss is celebrated for her pioneering work in the field of energy medicine and human consciousness. Her book *Anatomy of the Spirit*, one of the most important sources on energetic healing, explores the spiritual, emotional and psychological origin of all illness, and shows how to heal physical ailments once you realize their origins. Caroline has developed her ability to scan a person's circuitry—a person's mental, emotional, psychological, and spiritual currents of energy—to detect blockages in the energy centers, or chakras.

Her diagnostic intuition, sharp as a surgeon's scalpel, helps her identify the psychological and emotional factors hidden in her client's energy field that compromise perfect health. Through intuitive diagnosis, she adroitly tunes into and interprets this electromagnetic information and translates it into insights, remedies, and lifestyle recommendations. Pancreatic disorders such as diabetes, for example, often reflect responsibility issues for the individual being diagnosed. For instance, when a child perceives one or both parents as requiring parenting, the toxic energy of resentment builds up, attacking the pancreas and destabilizing the insulin production needed to regulate blood-sugar levels.

Various physical illnesses correlate to very specific patterns of emotional and psychological stress. For example, financial fears and stress characteristically affect the lower back, whereas emotional blockages such as an inability to receive or feel love often impact the heart and circulatory system.

Reprogramming old patterns of thought and emotion that create illness can restore a person to vibrancy. Caroline scans her client's aura, or energy field (the magnetic envelope surrounding and permeating the physical body). This scan provides revealing information about the person's emotional/psychological conflicts and patterns that may be feeding a medical problem. For example, one may receive an image or a strong impression that a person's lower spine is "like concrete." The medical correlation might be a slipped disc or a pinched nerve in the lower spinal area.

With practice you can learn to do an intuitive X ray or body scan on yourself or others to detect physical ailments, diagnose their emotional/psychological roots, and intuit the pathway to healing. These are the three steps you will learn in the intuitive energetic-healing techniques of scanning.

A PRIMER FOR USING YOUR X-RAY VISION

As a preamble to learning the scan, recall in Chapter 3 how the creative imagery group entered their inner diagnostic chamber to scan for troubled areas for Jorge. Many in this group learned how to do body scans as part of their training in the Silva Method, which teaches people to enter the alpha state—a creative brain-wave frequency—to have access to and magnify their intuitive powers. Norma De Armon, the leader, reads to the group a person's name, location, age, and physical description, including his or her height, weight, and eye and hair color. Then the body scan process begins.

There are many ways of doing a scan. When I do a scan, I imagine the outline of a body with the face turned to me. I look to see if any dark or gray spots appear in the outline. Then I turn the body around and look for any discoloration. Since my inner *hearing* is highly developed, sometimes I hear the name of a condition called out to me. My husband, Jim, on the other hand, scans the body and *sees* the dis-eased area appear in the color red or orange. I watched Norma one night and noticed that she did the scan with her eyes closed, her hand raised as it rose up through this imaginary body, looking for areas of heat.

The scan that I will direct you through covers the front and back view simultaneously. All you need in order to do this scan, aside from putting yourself in a quiet setting where you will not be disturbed, is the belief that you *can* do it and the willingness to give your full attention to the task at hand.

PRACTICE: DOING A BODY SCAN

Again, I suggest that you put the directions for this body scan on a cassette tape or let someone read them to you. If that is not possible, then first get a sense of the body you are going to visualize once you are settled into your quiet space.

Find a time when you will be undisturbed for fifteen minutes and go to your Mindshift Area. Get into a comfortable position. Close your eyes and take three deep breaths. Feel the air as it comes in and goes out. Notice and release any physical discomfort. Relax on every level. Notice any thoughts passing through your mind or any emotions distracting you. Tell these thoughts and feelings that you will attend to them later but don't want to be disturbed right now.

Now imagine the outline of the person's body you want to scan. Any or all of the following intuitive indicators might surface. You might notice gray or dark areas. You might be aware of sensations of cold or heat. There might be areas of color, such as red or orange.

Starting at the top of the head, scan the forehead, eyebrows, eyes, nose, mouth, cheeks, chin, and lips of the image. Notice if any tension is being held in the jaw. Scan into the back of the head along the scalp and hairline. Move into the throat, the front and back of the neck, and the point where the neck connects to the body. Scan the area between the shoulders and the head. Be aware of the spinal column. Move your awareness into the shoulder blades, upper back, and collarbone. Let your scan stream down into the upper arms on the right and left, to the elbows, forearms, wrists, and fingers. Then return to the chest area and explore the heart region. Now move to the rib cage and the sides of the body. Do you sense any tension in this body?

Scan through the solar plexus and stomach area, into the lower part of the body, the lower back, buttocks, and abdomen, down into the genitals, groin, hips, thighs, through the nerve fibers, blood vessels, fatty tissues, muscles, skin, and bones; then down into the upper legs, calves, shins, kneecaps, knee joints, and the soft fleshy areas behind the knees. Finally, go down to the right foot and then the left foot, noticing the toes, balls of the feet, arches, and heels.

If you had a checklist in front of you, would any of these areas become illuminated in your mind's eye? Brain, throat, lungs, heart, stomach, pancreas, spleen, gallbladder, liver, kidney(s), bladder, small intestine, large intestine, reproductive system, circulatory system, nervous system, muscular system, glandular system, skeletal system.

The areas that caught my attention on the scan are _____

_____

_____

_____

_____

What I noticed about these areas was _____

_____

_____

_____

_____

Did any images or thoughts come to you, suggesting what the dis-ease might be telling the person? _____

_____

_____

_____

In the next section, you will see how physical dysfunctions are induced and influenced by many factors, including emotional attitudes, beliefs, and experiences that we acquire during our life.

CONDUCTING THE BODY SYMPHONY

Smiling, the diminutive dynamo Ilana Rubenfeld enters the seminar room and is soon surrounded by people. She is here to teach body-workers how to develop a "listening touch" that will help their clients connect with the bound-up emotions crying out for expression in their physical ailments. For example, Ilana feels the tension in a person's knee and intuitively senses that the distressed person wants to stay locked in place rather than advance on the job. She then leads the client on a body/mind journey, first exploring current sensations and emotions, then investigating their roots in the past, and finally returning with new resources to cope in the present and heal physical distress. In this process, the listening touch is vital for restoring the body, mind, heart, and soul to harmony. "The body is our instrument," Ilana says, "and we need to listen to its song." This insight is the underlying metaphor of her healing path.

The Past: Once Upon a Time
At five years old, Ilana Rubenfeld moved from Israel to Manhattan. Speaking only Hebrew in an Irish-Catholic neighborhood made

her vigilant in many ways. Regular beatings by children in the neighborhood honed her intuition, sensitizing her to nonverbal cues foreshadowing danger. Her intuition became so highly developed that she knew people's intentions before they acted.

As a young musician, she studied with Pablo Casals and eventually became an orchestral and choral conductor and an assistant to Leopold Stokowski. Then a debilitating back spasm struck, forcing her to reorchestrate her life. But Ilana the musician birthed Ilana the bodyworker; her hands and all her senses now became her instrument, and her patients were the compositions she explored and interpreted.

The Present: Rubenfeld Synergy Method

The Rubenfeld Synergy Method (RSM), a powerful holistic system, integrates body, mind, emotions, and spirit by incorporating elements of the Alexander Technique, the Feldenkrais Method, Gestalt practice, and Ericksonian hypnotherapy into a blend of intuitive touch and psychotherapy.

Ilana discovered that neither bodywork nor psychotherapy could address the whole person. So, this visionary pioneer combined all these methods together in a synergistic approach. Practitioners of RSM listen with their hands to the body, whose stories, often from as far back as early childhood, must be "heard" for healing to occur. Using gentle touch with verbal dialogue, RSM practitioners access emotions and memories stored in the client's body that cause energy blocks, tensions, and imbalances. By using active imagination and visualization, the client relives the experience in real time, reviews the past, resolves unfinished business, and integrates new insights into the present. Thus somatic and emotional change is experienced in the present and embedded in the nervous system. In RSM, the present becomes the client's life in miniature.

The Gentle Touch

Now let's focus on this gentle touch, where the hands also become the eyes and ears. Ilana recommends a featherlight listening touch, which she calls noodling, to get to those feelings that have caused a person to be tight or tense. One might touch a shoulder or an arm or gently guide a client through a series of slow movements, rolling the head, shifting limbs, paying attention to the spine, and noticing the body's limits. As one's listening hands become more intuitive, they can sense blocked areas of the body that may be holding traumatic memories, identifying areas of physical tightness and injury, and intuiting the issues that underlie these conditions. This begins a dialogue between the client's cognitive mind, body, and emotions, which the client may carry on with the tense area by giving it a voice.

Does this sound familiar? In an exercise at the beginning of this chapter, you engaged in a dialogue with an ailing bodily part to discover the issues underlying its condition. When a person works through feelings and memories connected to an ailing body part, its quality of energy changes markedly. An area once physically tight becomes alive and pulsating, as the muscles become soft and relaxed.

With practice, our listening hands can accurately sense, receive, and interpret information stored in the human body. Touch directly links the cell consciousness of both client and bodyworker. Through touch, you listen to the body tell its truth. A person may verbally speak one version of reality while his or her body tells another story reflecting the authentic state. For example, one woman insisted that she had forgiven her father's abuse, while her body exhibited a steel-like rage.

Your listening hands heighten a person's awareness of the area that is being touched. The important moment is when the person becomes conscious enough to let go of the tension and emotion, rather than unconsciously holding on to it.

This intuitive touch links you with a person's cell consciousness and can facilitate or trigger healing. Intentional touch combined with movement creates a dialogue between a patient, his or her body, and the unconscious mind. Touching with the intent to heal builds a bridge to a person's neuromuscular system, which in turn gives feedback about the state of his or her body/mind. The following is a technique that Ilana uses to experiment with intentionality. This exercise demonstrates how our thoughts and feelings affect the way we experience touch.

PRACTICE: AN EXPERIENCE WITH INTENTIONAL TOUCH

Find a partner and stand at his or her side, facing his or her left shoulder. Have your partner close his or her eyes and stand quietly. Imagine that something is wrong with your partner's left shoulder and that you must *do something* quickly to fix it. Now touch your partner as you think this thought. After a few moments, move your hands away and rest them at your sides. Be quiet for a few seconds. Now imagine that the shoulder before you belongs to a healthy person and that your intention is *not* to do something quickly to fix it. Instead, your attitude is one of not doing, of allowing a change to emerge at its own pace. Now touch your partner's shoulder with that intention of *allowing* rather than *doing*. While you remain focused in this attitude, allow your partner the time and space to release any tensions (in his or her back and neck). You may feel a distinct shift in the quality and texture of your partner's shoulder. Now slowly move your hands away from your partner and let them rest at your sides. Walk around so that you are facing your partner. Ask your partner to open his or her eyes slowly. Notice any changes that have occurred in your partner's facial expression, breathing pattern, and entire body.

What was it like to touch your partner? _____
_____
_____

What was it like for your partner to be touched with these two different intentions? _____
_____
_____

Record what you have both observed or learned from this exchange. _____
_____
_____
_____

The Clientele

All victims, whether battered women, children of alcoholics, victims of sexual abuse or war, survivors of the Holocaust, and children of survivors, carry memories of their trauma, their anxiety and horror, embedded in their flesh. Such people can talk about their traumas endlessly, but until they have released them on a cellular (somatic) level, their bodies suffer the effects.

Ilana illustrates this by the following example: "I touched a spot on the spine of a Holocaust survivor I was working with and she got very upset. I asked her to go back to find out what that was. In a dialogue, her spine said, 'I feel crushed in.' It turned out that in order to survive, for months and months, she and her family lived crushed together in a hole in the ground under a trapdoor. She was a baby then and is now in her forties. She had held the pain in her spine all this time."

The easiest client to work with is the person who has the courage to risk going through his or her dark shadows and also journey to his or her bright, joyful place. The toughest clients are those who don't want to take responsibility for their actions and continually blame others for their dilemmas.

Mind Your Body

Here is one last practice from Ilana Rubenfeld designed to release the tension and rigidity caused by memories and emotions buried in our bodies. The most common areas of stored tension are the upper back and neck.

1. Go to your Mindshift area and sit in a chair, with both feet on the ground and your back away from the back of the chair so you are not leaning against it.
2. Roll your eyes to the right and then let your neck and body follow as far as you can go.
3. When you can't go any farther, take a mental photograph of that spot. Don't push yourself; just turn gently to the right, stop when it becomes a strain, and mark the spot visually.
4. Come back to the front and gently close your eyes.
5. Take your left hand, pass it over the top of your head, and cover your right ear.

6. Now lean gently to the left. Do it in a quiet, soft way, as if you're a beautiful bamboo tree swaying in the breeze. Use your imagination.
7. Bend gently to the left side several times, then return to the middle. Become aware of what your body is doing. Begin to listen to your ribs . . . neck . . . spine.
8. Let all that go . . . and now take your right hand and pass it over the top of your head and cover your left ear.
9. Now bend a few times to the right. Imagine again that you're a bamboo or a lovely plant waving in the wind. Think soft, and use whatever images work for you.
10. Next, take several deep breaths and come back to the middle.
11. Take your left hand once again and pass it over the top of your head and cover the right ear.
12. This time roll your eyes to the left and twist around as if you're looking at someone behind you, then come back to the front again.
13. Now when you twist again to the left, look out of the right corners of your eyes to the right. In other words, twist in one direction and look in the opposite direction.
14. Come back to the front and let everything go, returning your arms to your sides.
15. Now go back to steps 2 and 3 of this practice—roll your eyes to the right and let your head, neck, and body also twist to the right as far as you can. How far can you turn now? Did you pass the original spot that you visually marked?
16. Return to the middle and notice how your back, neck, and head feel.

Appreciate your new freedom and enjoy!

Chapter Eight

A View from the Healers

If you accept the premise that we are all responsible for our own healing, then it follows that we are all healers. We generally bestow that title not on ourselves but on a select group of people who have a listening touch, "special" healing powers, or perhaps simply medical degrees. In this chapter, you will meet four body/mind specialists who heal using the intuitive powers of their inner physicians. And you will hear their healing wisdom, which can help you restore yourself to wholeness.

Any change introduced at any level of the being affects every other level and the equilibrium of the whole person. This fundamental insight explains the nature of the body/mind connection and points the way to true healing.

Now it's time to focus on what actually constitutes a healing. But first let's explore what the word "healing" means to you.

PRACTICE: A HEALING PROBE

Ask yourself, "What does the word healing mean?" Write down everything that comes to your mind. Let the words, phrases, or sentences associated with this word flow out, and record them below. _____

_____

_____

_____

_____

Now put down your pen or pencil and become very still. Take a deep breath and relax; release any nagging thoughts or emotions that may be crying out for attention. Enter into a deeper level of consciousness to explore what healing means to you. Take five to seven minutes for this practice. Then record your insights here. _____

_____

_____

_____

_____

If I asked ten health-care professionals about what the word "healing" means, I might get ten different replies. Yet beneath apparent differences are commonalities. "Illness" suggests something amiss in the psyche or the body. "Healing" is the restoration of harmony or wholeness. Both the inner and the outer being must be addressed. Imagine a car going forty miles an hour that hits a telephone pole. Of course the *exterior* of the car must be cosmetically repaired, but so must the engine and other operating circuits *inside* the car. A mechanic won't stop at the car's outer shell, but will go inside the car to restore it to wholeness again. And the driver will also want to consider his own performance in order to avoid future accidents. So it is with the repair of human dis-ease. We must treat the whole person, not just the physical symptoms or surface ailments. True healing occurs when physical symptoms are treated in conjunction with emotional, mental, and spiritual adjustments. Only then can the person be restored to wholeness.

Any dis-ease, pain, illness, or dysfunction is like a red flare warning of danger ahead, of something out of balance in the body/mind. A wise outer physician encourages you to engage your inner physician's help in restoring your health. The healers profiled below offer several such ways to reestablish wholeness.

A PRIMER: WHY ILLNESS INCAPACITATES

Dr. Hanna Nathans, who lives in the Netherlands, is a certified management consultant and trainer, and also an intuitive reader and healer. Through her extensive practice in consulting and coaching individuals and organizations, Hanna has developed some remarkable insights on healing. For Hanna, healing is not simply a matter of push the right button and the ailment disappears. First, the question "Why are we ill?" must be asked. Too often, people want to banish the symptoms without first determining the cause of the malady. Hanna knows there are many nonphysical reasons underlying the manifestation of illnesses and accidents. Of course, on a conscious level, you don't want to be ill. But on a subconscious level your deeper self is urgently communicating through physical ailments.

Hanna speaks of a higher and lower consciousness within the subconscious. The lower consciousness contains childhood survival strategies, primal impulses and drives, character fixations, and vitality. The higher consciousness guides one's course in life and is a matrix of moral awareness, spiritual connection, and inspiration. According to Hanna, the lower consciousness is shortsighted like a child; it directs you away from pain or toward pleasure in the short term. This lower consciousness urges you toward safety and away from risk, which can also mean short-term security over long-term growth—as in a work situation where you might accept chronic stress and make no effort to resolve it for fear of losing your job. Sometimes your lower consciousness guides you to hit first so you are not hit. It tries to protect you from real or imagined dangers, such as rejection, criticism, loss of control, loss of face, and loss of love. And it may continue to use in your adulthood the strategies that succeeded when you were a child.

Often we don't heed the advice from the subconscious to slow down, relax, or take a break. If we ignore stress, fatigue, or overwork too long, the subconscious is not above taking drastic measures to get our attention.

A friend of mine was putting in long days as the manager of a busy clothing store. She refused to delegate responsibility to others, believing she had to do everything herself. She began suffering from chronic headaches and had no personal life. Still she refused to slow down. Finally, the inevitable happened. She fell off the stockroom ladder and knocked herself out on the cement floor. She spent several days recovering from the accident. Wouldn't a nice weekend off have been preferable?

Reflect on your own life. How often have you been forced to rest by illness after ignoring warning signals from the subconscious? Perhaps you got the flu when the stress in the office became overwhelming. When you are ill and being cared for, you are finally getting the nurturing you deny yourself when you are healthy. You take a necessary and healing break from your responsibilities. But illness is a last resort, and we can find ways to take breaks in our busy lives *before* illness occurs. Hanna emphasizes that most people don't consciously *choose* to become ill. The subconscious, acting as a protector or guardian angel, steers the body onto this illness course, to spare the individual greater trouble down the line. For many of us, if illness never forced us to rest and rejuvenate, we might literally work ourselves to death.

The Learning Annex

The inner physician resides in our higher consciousness, according to whose broader view today's pain may become tomorrow's gain. From this perspective, illness is, on the subconscious level, *chosen* as a way of learning. Illness or injury may evoke in us feelings of rebellion, resistance, rage, and grief. "Why me?" is a common refrain. Note, however, a subconscious choice to become ill does not mean that when someone is sick, it is his or her fault. Illness offers an opportunity for growth just as relationships, talents, and careers also grow through periods of crisis. Hanna says, "Illness has a function for us or it contains a lesson." And we must learn the lesson, she says, or the problem of illness will repeat itself. The lessons may include learning to speak up, to relax, to be more responsible or independent, or to let go of superficialities.

A serious illness often causes a redirection of energy and a shifting of priorities. Excessive burnout forced one workaholic finance manger to reorient his priorities. He had to let go of his excessive striving for status, money, and power. His stress-induced illness forced him to rethink what he really wanted in life, and he became a counselor for managers who also wanted to reorient their lives and careers.

Instead of getting the flu when stress in the office becomes overwhelming, nurture yourself instead by applying the proactive health measures from Chapter 6 and saying no to overwork. Debilitating illnesses caused by stress can be avoided through proactive measures. Examine the stress-producing patterns you may unconsciously engage in. These may include excessive perfectionism or competitiveness or passive submission to abuse. You can overcome perfectionism by cultivating the attitude that "my best effort is good enough." You can transcend any unhealthy attitude by recognizing the suffering it causes and consciously cultivating a new and healing attitude in its place. An overly competitive person who continually strives against others will find himself or herself lonely not only at the top but wherever he or she goes. To recognize this illness-producing attitude gives one the option to shift to cooperation and harmony with others, to see *this* as success. Healthy attitudes are an essential foundation of healthy bodies, minds, and spirits.

The Healing Touch

Hanna tells a poignant story about the famous grief therapist, Elisabeth Kübler-Ross. One of Kübler-Ross's patients, a young child with cancer, hung on to life for a long time, surviving in agony. The suffering child was able to die only when her mother said it was all right for her to go. The moral of this story is that not everything and everyone can or should be healed. When the inner physician or higher consciousness has chosen the way of a fatal disease, it is not easy for the surviving relatives to understand. And it is not always best to keep trying to cure a dying person. Why would we want our loved ones to remain alive when their joy and the quality of their life has slipped away?

PRACTICE: CREATING IMAGERY FOR HEALING

Before you do the following healing practice, Hanna suggests that you engage in a silent conversation with your inner physician, to understand the reasons for the dis-ease and determine whether and how you are allowed to intervene.

If you are doing a healing for someone else, keep a clear separation between that person and yourself. You don't want to absorb the unhealthy energy of the other person! A way to guard against this is to picture the other person and imagine a rose between the two of you. The rose filters the energy that goes back and forth between you.

After receiving consent to do a healing, you can do any or all of the following practices.

First, become receptive, slow down your breathing, and do a relaxation exercise. Next, the person and the dis-eased spot need to be grounded. There are many ways to do this. One way is to draw an imaginary line from the person's tailbone to the dis-eased spot and then down to the center of the earth. Imagine that you are writing today's date and the name of the person on that line.

Using your imagination, change the line into a tube. Let the bad energy flow down to the center of the earth, where it is neutralized and purified. Now imagine a sun shining above your head, filling you with endless light and pure energy. Let this healing energy flow through you into the other person, filling the space where the bad energy used to be.

What sensations do you feel from doing this practice? _____

_____

_____

_____

Now imagine a rose. Move it around the location of the dis-ease. Imagine it slurping out all the bad energy. Throw the imaginary rose away or let it evaporate outside your aura or the magnetic field surrounding your body. Let the transformed energy flow back into your sun. Fill the space left when the bad energy is pulled out with the energy from your own sun.

What sensations do you feel from doing this exercise? _____

_____

_____

_____

You can also imagine divine or healing energy from the cosmos going directly to the spot and healing it. What sensations do you feel from this healing imagery? _____

_____

_____

Use your imagination to go to a part of your body or to a part of the other person's body, be it an ankle, a leg, the lungs, or whatever

needs healing. Imagine that the area you are focusing on is functioning and completely well. See and feel this as vividly as you can. You
may need to repeat this again at several other sittings.

Can you feel that area becoming more energized? _____

_____

_____

To end, stabilize your healing by saying an affirmation. For example, "My ankle is healed now and functioning properly." Or you
can end with an image that reinforces the healing, such as imagining
the foot being put into a healing bath.

Record your healing experiences, focusing on a particular part of
the body. _____

_____

_____

_____

THE FAMILY PHYSICIAN SPEAKS TO THE INNER PHYSICIAN

Dr. Gladys McGarey is internationally known through her world-
wide lectures, her writing, and her pioneering work in natural birthing and holistic medicine.

I saw Dr. Gladys, as she is affectionately known, give the keynote
address to a huge audience at a conference. Can you imagine my
excitement when she began her address by saying that true healing
doesn't happen unless the doctor and patient contact their inner
physicians? Dr. Gladys describes the electric charge that fills the
examining room when patients realize they are in charge and can
actually affect their own healing. Then, Dr. Gladys says, the outer
physician can become part of the patient's team, assisting the physician within each patient.

A Cure Is Not a Healing

Dr. Gladys emphasizes the difference between cures and healing.
She feels that *cures* patch things up, while *healing* changes the condition from the inside out. She replaces the word "wellness" with

"wholeness," because many sick people may become whole, yet never get over their illness. For example, she treated a sick woman who spent hours idly looking at the door from her hospital bed. One day the woman noticed a cross on the door and felt Jesus Christ come over and heal her. Amazed, she asked Christ, "How did you manage to get off the cross, come over here, and go back again?" The one-word reply she heard was "Velcro." Although the patient never became well, Dr. Gladys points out that she became whole, because she died in peace, her sense of humor intact and in contact with the divine.

I know people who have suffered one catastrophic illness after another who proudly show off their scars and brag about their hospital stories. Yet they return to the hospital again and again because they never look beneath the surface to discover the underlying cause of their illnesses.

Dr. Gladys knows from her fifty years as a family physician the necessity of a patient contacting the inner physician in order to effect a true healing. One patient who lived some distance away from Dr. Gladys was quite upset when another physician diagnosed her with a bladder infection. The patient had a gut feeling that this diagnosis was wrong and wanted a second opinion from Dr. Gladys. But when she was unable to contact Dr. Gladys, she imagined a conversation in which Dr. Gladys asked her, "What do you think is going on?" Then the patient checked herself intuitively and sensed that she was suffering from a vaginal infection, not a bladder infection. She returned and told her intuition to the original doctor, who examined her again and discovered that her intuitive diagnosis was correct. The patient's inner physician gave the right message.

The Prescription for Connecting Within

Dr. Gladys's prescriptions for connecting with the inner physician include physical touch (massage, for example), dreamwork, and healing affirmations.

One way to connect with the inner physician is through physical contact—allowing ourselves to be touched. For instance, Dr. Gladys suggests that women check their breasts regularly by touching them and saying, "Hi, girls. How are you? Do you have a message for me?" This positive, playful attitude brings an automatic body response. Don't be afraid to check and have contact with your body.

Bodywork such as osteopathic and chiropractic manipulation is very healing. Massage is another great way of contacting the inner physician, who in turn activates the emotional memories locked in your body. Dr. Gladys tells of a truck driver who came to her clinic with lung cancer and directed his rage at everyone and everything. This continued for five days. The moment of transformation came when this big angry guy sat down after a massage, tears streaming down his face. When he composed himself, he shared the following story. When the therapist touched his feet, something opened up above him. He became aware of a light pouring through him. When the therapist touched his chest, he said he felt the saintly hands of Christ touching him. The inner healing triggered by this massage allowed him to live the remaining two months of his life differently and to die a changed person.

PRACTICE: REACH OUT AND TOUCH

You can find many wonderful books on massage in any bookstore. Set aside an evening to exchange massages with a spouse, lover, or friend. You can even give yourself a massage. Do this for at least twenty minutes after entering a relaxed, intuitive state. How did the healing touch through the massage help you connect with the physician within? _____

_____
_____
_____
_____

Does your inner physician have a specific message about how to care for your body? What other message are you getting? _____

_____
_____
_____
_____

Arrange a healing appointment with a professional bodywork practitioner (that is to say, a massage therapist, a chiropractor, or someone doing Rolfing, Rosen, or Alexander) for the purpose of contacting your inner physician. How did you feel after this body-work session? _____

_____

_____

_____

_____

Dreams are another way to contact the physician within. Dr. Gladys tells of a patient who could not find relief from her painful headaches. Then the patient told Dr. Gladys the following dream. In the dream the patient took from her purse what she thought were pain pills. Then Dr. Gladys came in and said, "Don't take that." The patient looked down and saw she was holding M & M candies. When Dr. Gladys heard this dream she realized that the patient was sneaking chocolate in real life, believing that if Dr. Gladys didn't know, it would be all right. The patient was able to fool her outer physician, but not the physician within who diagnosed her allergy to chocolate as the cause of her headache.

The power of affirmations is illustrated by the case of an eighty-seven-year-old woman with a strong aversion to doctors. She had avoided seeing a doctor for sixty-seven years and didn't want to be put in the hospital. She finally visited Dr. Gladys due to a sizable lump in her breast. The old woman told Dr. Gladys she'd had the lump for a decade or so! She said that whenever it began to grow, she simply told it to stop growing. As a result, she had effectively managed a tumor that should have killed her years before.

Hearing this, Dr. Gladys challenged her to use this power of affirmation to make the lump go away. Six months later, she returned to the examining room; the mass was much smaller. Within two years the tumor was almost gone. The fearless octogenarian said, "I got tired of fussing with it and said, 'That thing will never kill me. It wouldn't dare.' " And it didn't, thanks to her iron will.

The Support System

During the fourteen years I lived in the Midwest, I had the joy of watching the geese fly over our lake on their journey south. I enjoyed reading the scientific explanations of why geese fly in a V formation.

Dr. Gladys sees the flight patterns of geese as important metaphors for human community and support systems.

She says, "As each bird flaps its wings, it creates an uplift for the bird immediately following. By flying in a V formation, the whole flock adds at least 71 percent greater flying range than if each bird flew alone." For Dr. Gladys, the lesson is that people who share a common direction and create community by cooperative networking can get where they are going easier and faster because their collective power is far greater than the sum of their individual efforts.

Another fact is that whenever a goose falls out of formation, it suddenly feels the drag and resistance of flying alone and quickly gets back into formation to take advantage of the lifting power of the bird immediately in front. As Dr. Gladys says, "If we have as much sense as a goose, we will stay in formation with those who have headed where we want to go and be willing to accept their help as well as extend help to all others."

Also, when the lead goose gets tired, it rotates back in the formation and another goose flies up to the point position. The lesson learned from this is that "it pays to take turns doing the harder task, sharing leadership with others."

And did you know that the geese in formation honk from behind to encourage those up front? We also need to be sure our "honking from behind" is encouraging, not something else.

Finally, when a goose gets sick or is wounded, two geese drop out of formation to help it and protect it. They stay with it until it is able to fly again or dies. Then they link up on their own with another formation or catch up with their flock. Says Dr. Gladys, "If we have as much sense as geese, we too will stand by each other in difficult and stressful times as well as when we are strong."

For the sake of our health and wholeness, all of us, no matter what our chosen work, need a community and support system.

PRACTICE: THE GEESE LESSONS

How can you apply the five geese lessons to your life? _____

_____

_____

_____

_____

_____

_____

CONNECTING WITH THE LIFE ENERGY

Karen Kramer is a body/mind psychologist who has developed an expertise in Qi Gong (pronounced *chee goong*), a form of energy therapy and massage developed many centuries ago in China. "Qi" means breath, spirit, energy of life, and "Gong" means skill, practice, or work—work with the life energy, breath, and spirit. Karen combines psychotherapeutic practice with Qi Gong to help clients release energy blockages that cause illness, inhibit relationships, and impede goal achievement and success.

The ancient Chinese Taoist monks discovered energy surrounding all living things and began to harness and move this vital energy within themselves through movement, breath, imagery, and concentration. The goal they sought was not only health but longevity, and even immortality. They learned to extend the Qi beyond their bodies and cultivated extraordinary abilities and healing powers. The practices in this book that involve breathing, relaxation, and visualization or "imaging" are in fact contemporary Qi Gong healing practices based on the same ancient principles.

Qi Gong's Healing Power

Qi Gong practice yields innumerable benefits. It accounts for the Taoist Qi Gong masters' fame for living a century and more in a state of dynamic, radiant health. Qi Gong is an ancient energy system that draws in, conducts, and directs the life energy through the body for physical healing and rejuvenation and the cultivation of higher spiritual and psychic abilities. In ordinary life, Qi is drawn into the body through the breath with every inhalation. This life force is stored in the lower belly, also known as the dantian or the hara, the body's central sun, and radiated throughout the body. The Qi is also distributed through the circulatory system via the blood and the nervous system.

Qi Gong practice enhances the circulatory system by mentally stimulating the bodily areas through imagining techniques. And it oxygenates the body via conscious or intentional breathing. Since Qi Gong exercises are performed in the relaxed or intuitive state you have been learning in this book, it reduces hypertension and calms the nervous system. The act of concentration by which these techniques are accomplished literally puts the mind in the body, filling it with consciousness, or light. The circulation of the Qi bathes and stimulates the entire body and all its various centers and organs with the radiant life force that sustains us. Every area of the body is affected; thyroid and immune functioning are improved, the elimination of toxins is accelerated, and mental functioning and clarity are heightened. Qi Gong practice, like yoga or mediation, can also transform anger, depression, or anxiety into clarity, calmness, and a sense of well-being.

Keep in mind that we already have this Qi within us. Qi Gong simply amplifies and conducts this power by conscious intention using specific techniques, drawing greater energy into our systems and conducting it through our whole beings, from our bones and muscles to the subtlest levels of our psycho-physical circuitry.

I will now teach you a simple and powerful Qi Gong exercise that builds on the skills you have already begun to develop through the practices in this book, which are themselves a kind of Qi Gong, or spirit-energy exercise. This exercise, which illustrates the basic principles of Qi Gong, can be applied to every kind of healing with remarkable results.

PRACTICE: THE RADIANT INNER SUN

Sit erect with your hands resting on your thighs or in your lap. Close your eyes, relax your body, and take three deep, slow breaths. Now feel your hara (again, in your lower belly, beneath the belly button) as a ball of radiant energy, which it is. Imagine that it is the center of life, the pulsing energy core at the heart of the entire universe. Now, take seven total breaths, as described in Chapter 6, and with each breath, perform the following Qi Gong exercise. As you inhale directly into your hara, feel it glow and light up as a live coal does when you blow on it. Feel the energy of the universe drawn in through every pore in your body, through all your muscles, tissues, organs, and bones, directly into your hara. That is what causes your solar plexus to glow and light up: inhaling the energy of the universe, saturating your entire being with Qi in the process.

When your inhale is complete, begin your exhale, and as you do, focus again on your hara. Feel the force of your exhalation blowing through your hara, which now lights up like a sun, sending its rays through the entire body, illuminating it with white or golden light. Both feeling and imagery powerfully enhance the circulation of the Qi through the body/mind. So feel and see this inner sun magnified by your exhalation, radiating a bright and living energy outward through your entire body/mind, purifying, rejuvenating, and saturating every cell with healing light.

You can turn this into a dynamic energizing practice very simply. Any time you feel tired or mentally sluggish, perform this exercise standing up. But when you have inhaled a total breath, hold it in and tense or clench your entire body from head to toe for a count of three seconds, feeling the Qi energizing and stimulating your entire body, brain, and nervous system. Then exhale and relax your body, feeling the energy radiate outward from the hara. Do this seven times and notice the dramatic increase in your mental alertness and physical energy.

How do you feel after doing this practice? _____

Qi Gong Healing

Now we will use this simple Qi Gong technique and apply it to healing. It can be used for any illness, accident, or physical affliction, from headaches, bruises, and sprained ankles to heart conditions, organ malfunctions, and even cancer. You can also use it as a way to stimulate and energize the various organs of your body for increased health. Through the following practice, you will learn to saturate any part of yours or another's body with Qi, the life energy. There is no possibility of negative side effects; only good can result.

Now pick an injury you wish to heal or an organ you wish to simulate or strengthen. Perhaps you have a sprained ankle, a bad knee, or a weak heart. Sit in a comfortable chair, close your eyes, and enter the relaxed, intuitive state by taking three total breaths, using the Radiant Inner Sun technique just described. You are revving your Qi into high gear for maximum healing effect.

Now place both of your palms on the part of the body that you wish to heal or saturate with Qi. Keeping your eyes closed, perform the Radiant Inner Sun with the total breath. On the inhalation, see and feel the sun in your hara light up with powerful healing force. As you exhale, you will be directing this force in two ways.

First feel this light energy pour out of your hara in a living stream, directly into the intended area. If you are working on your kidneys, for example, then see and feel the stream of Qi pour from your hara directly into the kidneys. If you are working on a knee, leg, or ankle, see and feel the stream of Qi pour down through the limb into the specific area. As the energy pours into the organ or bodily area, see and feel it light up with Qi as a coal lights up when blown on.

At the same time, see and feel the energy rise out of the hara up through your heart, streaming through your shoulders and down both arms, to pour out of the palms of your hands and into the area you are working on. When you concentrate, you can actually feel the sensations of energy moving through your body, directed by your breath and attention. Again, imagine the area you are working on lighting up like a living coal. By sending the Qi into the intended area both directly from the hara and also up through the heart, down the arms, and out through your palms, you are completing a circuit and bombarding that area with a great amount of Qi, or healing life force.

You can also do these practice exercises at night in conjunction with any of the relaxation practices given in Chapter 6. While lying down in the relaxed state, simply direct the energy via imagery and breath from your hara into any area of your body, seeing and feeling the life force energizing and healing that area as it lights up like a glowing coal. Or simply breathe into the hara and radiate the Qi throughout your entire body on the exhale. Do either of these practices at least five minutes a day and notice the effects. What changes in your life energy do you notice after doing this exercise for one week? _____

_____

Qi Gong Head Massage

Throughout these exercises, be aware that the energy flow is going on at all times. The palms, the ears, and the soles of the feet have accupressure points for the entire body. So when you stimulate all those points, your entire system is bathed with nourishing energy from the Qi.

Dr. Kramer suggests doing the following head massage the first thing in the morning to stimulate mental clarity and activate the energy flow. As with the other Qi Gong exercises, do any one of these practices whenever you need the stimulation. For example, if you work at a computer and feel lethargic, stiff, or unfocused, do the neck rub described below. This relieves neck strain and increases the blood and oxygen flow to the brain.

Here are some exercises in Dr. Karen Kramer's Qi Gong head massage. Doing these practices in a series will stimulate all organ systems in three to five minutes. Each practice also has individual applications and can be performed for specific purposes.

PRACTICE: QI GONG HEAD MASSAGE

Prior to beginning, rub your hands together vigorously 36 times while gently shaking your lower belly or dantian. Shaking it stimulates the flow of Qi. The purpose of rubbing the hands together is to pull the Qi into the palms, which radiate the Qi. After rubbing your hands, rub the soles of your feet until both palms and soles feel warm. Now you are ready to begin the head massage.

> **Face Massage.** Starting at your chin, rub palms gently upward over the nose and face to the hairline, each palm circling out to the outer cheeks and back down, meeting at the chin. Breathe outward through the nose on the upstroke. Remember to keep the palms of the hands in contact with your face at all times. When you are stroking the face, you always want the palm to stay on the skin of the face. This gives the skin a lovely bath of Qi, reduces wrinkles, and makes you beautiful. Repeat this 36 times.
>
> **Back of Your Head.** Place your left hand with the palm down on the top of the head. With the right hand, rub the back of the

head over and just below the bony prominence using three fingers. Rub vigorously 60 times. Repeat that action with the right hand on the top of the head as you rub the bony prominence with the left hand, also 60 times. The palm that is placed on the top of your head is right over your immune center and is sending energy in from the fingers that are rubbing right down into that immune center under the palm. So you are getting a wonderful benefit by stimulating the immune center.

Over the Head.   Using three fingers on both hands, keep palms down, rub upward from the back of your neck along the rounded curve up to the bony prominence 50 times. You want to stimulate the energy paths that run along the middle of the scalp and just outside that midline.

Eye Exercises.   Warm each thumb by rubbing it vigorously on the opposite palm, then proceed with the eye wash: gently rub with the back of the warm thumb (area from the knuckle to nail) over the closed eyelid from nose to hairline, then rub below the eye. This is done 36 times. (Each stroke counts as one.)

Eye Workout.   Rub palms together until warm. Take the palms and place them over the closed eyes so that you can feel the eyes moving and roll the eyes in a circle to the left 9 times and in a circle to the right 9 times. Then move your eyes up and down 9 times and to the left and right 9 times. You want to put enough pressure on the eyes so they have to work against the palm of the hand. They are getting energy but they are also getting a little bit of a muscle workout, too. This practice refreshes your eyes. Also, you can simply rub your palms together, cup the eye, and send energy in.

Nose Rub.   Make fists with the hands, placing your thumbs side by side. Starting at the hairline, rub the back of your thumbs (area from the knuckle to nail) down beside the nose to and off the chin. Be sure to go straight down, exhaling with each stroke. Do this 36 times. Then place the index finger just below the outer edges of the nostrils, feeling the depression there. Massage counterclockwise 30 times. Finally, using the side of the index finger, briskly rub under the septum of the nose until it feels warm. This practice eases stuffiness from colds and relieves sinus congestion.

Ear Massage.   The ears, like the palms and soles of the feet, have acupoints that stimulate the major internal organs. This practice stimulates the flow of Qi through these organs and the entire body. Reach over the head with the right arm and grasp the top of your left ear. Gently pull up on the ear 36 times. Repeat with the right ear. Then grasp the fullest point of both ears, just above the lobe, and gently tug 36 times, away from the head. Finally, using the thumb and index finger, grasp the auricle, or shell, of the ear at the top where it joins the head and gently rub down over the entire auricle 36 times.

Beating the Heavenly Drum.   Create a light suction by placing the palms over the ears. With index fingers over middle fingers, snap the index fingers off the middle fingers against the hollow at the back of the head just below the bony prominence, 36 times. This practice can be used to inhibit tinnitus, or ringing in the ears, at any time. It also stimulates the hypothalamus, which is associated with the immune center.

Neck Rub.   Using the right palm first, vigorously rub the right side of the neck, just below the ear, 36 times. Repeat on the left side. Finally, alternating palms, rub gently down the throat from chin to collarbone 36 times. This stimulates the thyroid and aids in regulating body temperature. This is a good practice to do for re-energizing and mental alertness.

Scalp Massage.   Make your fingers into claws and vigorously rub over the scalp front to back, from the hairline to the nape of the neck, and at the sides of the head from the hairline to the nape. Each stroke counts as one. Repeat 36 times. This practice stimulates the scalp and promotes hair growth.

Knock Teeth.   Firmly knock your teeth together 36 times. Then, with mouth closed, run the tongue along the gums, outside the teeth, from right to left 9 times, then left to right 9 times. Next, run the tongue along the gums inside the teeth, 9 times to the left and 9 times to the right. The mouth will fill with saliva. Save it and swallow it after you have completed the gum massage. This saliva stimulates digestion. The entire practice strengthens and stimulates gums and teeth.

Record your experience after one week of doing the Qi Gong Head Massage. _____

_____

_____

_____

_____

_____

_____

_____

IGNITING THE CREATIVE FLOW

Alan Vaughan, an internationally known authority on intuitive phenomena, precognition, and prophetic dreams, has scientifically demonstrated his psychic skills by solving crimes and locating sunken ships. He offers a unique perspective on the purposes of illness and the nature of healing.

Alan feels that sometimes illness is a means used by individuals to make necessary lifestyle changes. He points out that many highly successful people have been transformed by incredible physical health challenges—a crisis thrust upon them, forcing them to go deep within and tap their spiritual reserves. In this way, illness or injury becomes a spiritual gift that allows them to connect with their higher self, the godlike consciousness within. In fact, every crisis offers the possibility of such transformation.

Another key insight of Alan's is the importance of creative participation in life, of having a goal for each day, a long-range vision etching one's life with a deep sense of purpose. A person who is spiritually aligned has a finely tuned immune system. This spiritual alignment is the natural result of a purposeful life lived in the creative mode. The healing power is ignited by creative activities such as writing and painting and by loving service to family, friends, and the world at large. Alan offers writer Anthony Burgess as a wonderful example of someone who used the healing power of creativity. Given a diagnosis of terminal cancer, Burgess ignored the doctors and wrote the book *Clockwork Orange* instead. Perhaps you will not be too surprised to hear the punch line—that Burgess's cancer was cured by the time he finished his book.

In the next practice, you will explore how your life is etched with a sense of purpose.

PRACTICE: EXPLORING YOUR LIFE PURPOSE

Take several minutes now to consider the following questions:
What do you think to be the purpose of your life? _____
_____
_____
_____

What are the things presently in your life that give you the most happiness or pleasure? _____
_____
_____

What gives you the greatest sense of energy, meaning, or accomplishment? _____
_____
_____

Is there anything you would strongly like or wish to do that you are not now doing? _____
_____
_____

Why aren't you doing it? List the reasons. _____
_____
_____

What practical steps could you take, even rearranging your life, that would allow you to live the life you would choose if you could?
_____
_____

Is it worth taking those steps? _____
_____
_____

If you never take them, will you regret it later on? _____
_____
_____

What do you choose to do? What is the first step you can take?
_____
_____
_____

Remember, perhaps the most powerful health strategy of all is living a purposeful life, doing the things you most love and give you the deepest sense of meaning. And like the journey of ten thousand miles, it often begins with a single step.

Chapter Nine

REVERSING A HEALTH
CHALLENGE TO CREATE
PERFECT HEALTH

B y now you know that you can be alive and enjoy radiant health if you visualize your body in that state, think healthy, energizing thoughts, feel self-confident, and claim the wholeness that is your spiritual birthright. The Mindshift workout in this chapter will help you figure out how to expand your perspective in order to deal with any highly stressful situation or debilitating health problem. You will see how such a change in consciousness will help you find meaning where before there seemed to be none, and will show you what steps to take next.

TURNING IT AROUND

There is a way out of any rut you have fallen into. "Accentuate the positive," turn your thoughts, feelings, and actions around, and adopt the attitude *I will become whole*. Your effort and energy can create the wholeness you desire.

Tag Yourself
Many years ago, I secretly harbored the desire to become a writer. I was a successful psychologist with many talents but would never

confess my heart's desire to anyone. Then I decided to *turn around* the belief that I couldn't write and make my dream come true. I started by *tagging* myself a writer. Every day I steadfastly affirmed "I am a writer." And I wrote something each day. My commitment to my goal and my vision of what I could be turned the tide. Before long, I had an article or two accepted for publication; then I went on to write many more articles and even a couple of books.

But the turning point came when I first tagged myself a writer. By my commitment and daily writing, I developed the inner quality necessary to make my dream a reality. And I continually affirmed my creativity and communication skills, making confidence and action my response to every doubt.

I now follow the same practice whenever I am ill, actively employing healing measures and affirming the desired outcome, knowing a positive mental attitude translates into physical healing. Attitude is the driver, and whichever way it steers, the body/mind will follow.

Right now, pick an inner quality you would like to develop and an outer goal you would like to accomplish. Prepare to turn what now seems unattainable into an actual accomplishment. Then tie this project into your desire for dynamic, optimal health.

What is your chosen goal? A trip to China? An African safari? To be a painter, writer, dancer? It must be something you truly desire, something you always thought you might do, if only. . . . So what is stopping you? The workaday obligations of life or the negative affirmation that you're too busy or tired or just can't do it?

Take a look at that old attitude and see if it's worth holding on to. If you could trade it in for a new, improved attitude that would support your dreams and help you turn what seemed unattainable into a reality, what would that attitude be? And what effect do you think it might have on your health?

PRACTICE: RADIATE AN INNER QUALITY

What inner quality or essence would you like to develop? Here are some *essence* suggestions that you might like to radiate and project like a fragrant perfume: integrity, purpose, clarity, peace, faith, willpower, transformation, inspiration, efficiency, enthusiasm, openness, harmony, balance, flexibility, understanding, courage, patience, adventure, joy, gratitude, trust, strength, release, humor, or honesty.

Pick two or three qualities you would like to radiate, qualities you will need to make your chosen goal become a reality. _____

_____

_____

For an entire day, stop at appropriate intervals and feel yourself radiating those qualities. You might also affirm "I have courage" or "I radiate harmony." At the same time, fix your mind on your goal and see what steps you will need to take to make it happen. Feel your goal magnify the qualities you are radiating and feel those qualities drawing you toward your goal. How do you feel after the day?

_____

_____

_____

On the second day, continue this practice, but also take one concrete step toward your goal. Do you notice an increased energy? Imagine if you continued this process, radiating new and positive attitudes as you made your dream come true. What effect do you think it would have on your health? _____

_____

_____

_____

Continue for one week and record your experiences at the end of that time. _____

_____

_____

_____

What do you think the connection is between attitude, goals, and radiant health? _____

_____

_____

_____

_____

Look for the Silver Lining

Once someone I loved very dearly fell into a deep clinical depression. I felt helpless and inadequate to save my companion, to guide him through the dark tunnel into the light. The refrain of an old spiritual came to my mind: "You got to walk that lonesome valley by yourself." A very dear psychologist friend would leave me E-mail messages filled with encouraging words, always painting a hopeful vision. As my companion sank deeper into despair, unable to receive my help, my psychologist friend would say, "I see that only good can come out of this acute depression." Reversing the situation, he envisioned my companion as whole, well, and magnificently transformed—a caterpillar becoming a beautiful butterfly. Inspired by his example, I also began, in the face of my companion's mental and physical deterioration, to affirm and believe that only good could come out of this. Perhaps my faith was more powerful than my attempts to help. A miraculous turnabout happened five months later, and the vision I had been affirming became a living reality.

In many cultures, illness or dis-ease is considered a time of learning, from which the individual emerges with greater wisdom. Illness forces us within. While I was writing a book on how successful people use intuition in decision-making, I interviewed an accomplished man who described his struggles with clinical depression. He knew that in this battle, where his life was at stake, he had to break through to something deeper than the narrow rationality he had been taught all his life or something essential in him would die. For him, the struggle forced him to trust a deeper part of himself that was calling him into a harmonious relationship with some larger whole. In calling upon this deeper level of reality, he learned to dance with the forces at play beyond himself and the conventional order he had mistaken for reality itself. He lauds his intuitive self for guiding him through this soul-wrenching struggle.

Perhaps darkness is an essential part of life, one of our inner seasons. It forces us to turn our perception around. I think we go down into the valley of despair in order to emerge with greater wisdom. From this perspective, every dark cloud does have its silver lining. In the next exercise, you will intuitively retrieve the lesson, or silver lining, hidden in one of your own discouraging times.

PRACTICE: LOOK FOR THE SILVER LINING

Find a time when you can go to your Mindshift Area and be quiet for at least twenty minutes. Take several deep breaths, relax into the intuitive state, and recall a time of darkness, depression, or despair. Affirm that you are on a treasure hunt, seeking the wisdom, strength, or shift—the silver lining—that came to you out of this experience. Engage in this deep introspection. What issues were you struggling with? What insights came to you? What was the turning point? What summary lesson did you learn? What positive quality or strength do you now have that you can trace to this experience? _____

_____

_____

_____

_____

From this experience, what pearl of wisdom would you share with someone else who is going through a discouraging time? _____

_____

_____

_____

_____

_____

MEET DR. FEELGOOD

An important step in reversing any health challenge is finding a way to saturate your everyday affairs with positive energy so that the dark areas of dis-ease are permeated by light. One way I gain this perspective is by calling on Dr. Feelgood.

Dr. Feelgood is my affectionate nickname for Sheba Penner, a dance therapist, hypnotherapist, and psychomotor therapist trained at New York Medical Center. Sheba coined the popular term "body language" back in 1968.

For the past thirty years, Sheba has helped countless individuals forge a connection between body, mind, emotion, and spirit. Through public workshops and private consultations, she skillfully guides people along the self-realization path to their full potential as co-creators with the Creative Force of the universe. According to Sheba, people who realize their full potential as dynamic and radiant beings will pass those same qualities on to others, who will follow suit—the domino theory of transformation.

Sheba believes that certain areas of our body are more vulnerable than other parts, and that genetic factors may make certain parts of the body more susceptible to dis-ease. She disagrees with those who claim that we totally create our reality and thereby attract cancer or paralysis. And she recognizes the error of blaming the victim by accusing people of creating their cancer or any other serious condition. Yet she acknowledges that predisposing psychological conditions, negative mental attitudes, and emotional states—in addition to an individual's genetic background—can be contributing factors to a dis-ease.

For instance, Sheba points to a common dynamic in which conscientious people devote themselves so exclusively to the needs of others that they fail to nurture themselves. This individual may unconsciously invite illness, so that he or she may receive the nurturing and care he or she has been subconsciously craving.

Our rapidly changing world challenges us to clarify our priorities: to choose how we want to live and to determine what matters most. Our health results from a constant balancing act between the demands of our external environment and the internal forces of our attitudes and thoughts. When you find this balance, you are not likely to be in dis-ease. Sheba sometimes equates illness with a wake-up call: "Are you in balance today?"

The Perfect Posture

The perfect inner posture for achieving and maintaining radiant health comprises several key elements: a loving acceptance of self; a strong intention to be healthy; and an ability to be still, open, and receptive to the input of your inner physician.

Becoming still allows you to be aware of your body and your thoughts and feelings, and to become spiritually aligned. The practice of loving self-acceptance begins by not judging yourself, not comparing yourself to others. The next step is realizing and affirming that you *deserve* to be healthy and happy and can *attract* whatever you need to make this your actual state. Over the years I have heard countless people say, "I want to be a loving person." You can't be a loving person unless you love yourself first. If you have not loved yourself for your entire adult life, simply reading these few sentences will not suddenly erase that past. But the following practice can help you learn to love yourself by allowing you to see yourself from a new perspective.

The Self as Other

You may have noticed that it seems easier to love and forgive others, especially children or those younger than you, than it is to love and forgive yourself. The following Mindshift meditation will give you a healing perspective.

PRACTICE: EMBRACING THE SELF AS OTHER

First, sit comfortably in a quiet place where you will not be disturbed, take several deep breaths, and bring yourself into the relaxed, intuitive state.

Now recall an early memory from childhood when you were in a state of innocence. Perhaps you were playing with friends or a pet, grieving over a childhood loss or wound, or basking in the attention of a parent or revered elder. If the child you were then were before you now, looking up to you in that state of innocence, how would you relate to him or her? You would probably embrace that child with warm and tender affection. So do this now in your imagination. Embrace the child you once were with love.

Now move ahead to your early teens. See yourself in that time of biological change and emotional upheaval. See how you struggled to make sense of the world, awkward and bewildered as the innocence of childhood vanished in the face of the complex social demands of adolescence. If the confused teenager you were then stood before you now, you would probably feel compassion for him or her and want to help him or her through this difficult life passage. Express this compassion to your former self now.

Now move ahead to a time in your twenties, when you were struggling to establish yourself as an adult in the world, hoping to succeed, to achieve some goal or fulfill a dream. Recall the ideals and the vision of life that inspired you. If that person were before you now, you would probably wish him or her every success and want his or her dreams to come true. Feel these feelings now for the person you were then.

Now imagine yourself ten or twenty years in the future. See yourself older, wiser, having learned many life lessons and matured far beyond your present state. See that older, wiser you looking back on the person you are now. How would that person look at you? With at least as much, if not more, tenderness, compassion, and loving acceptance as you felt looking back on your own past selves. Do you think your future self would want you to judge and criticize yourself harshly now?

Now embrace that wiser future self, who is in you now (or you would not be able to imagine him or her), and digest, internalize, and absorb this mature, healing perspective. The truth is that you can become that future self at any moment through this simple shift of perspective. Any time you notice that you are judging yourself harshly, withholding from yourself the love you deserve, make this shift and become your own guardian angel.

Record your experiences and revelations with each self. _____

_____

_____

_____

_____

_____

_____

The Body/Mind

When you become committed to your own healing, a process of discovery begins. You contain within yourself all the vital elements and wisdom this journey to wholeness requires. Your inner physician is there to provide intuitive diagnoses and remedies and to act as your guide. And you now have the Mindshift Method and all of its proactive and potent healing elements to give you access to and help you develop your natural intuitive gifts.

We will now do another powerful Mindshift practice based on Sheba's work and insights. Sheba emphasizes that we magnetize or draw to ourselves the same energies and qualities (in the form of people, experiences, and so on) that we nurture or cultivate within ourselves. Another way to put this comes in the form of an ancient Indian aphorism: "You become or attract to yourself whatever you meditate on." This means that if we are always fearful or angry, we will perceive life through these filters and draw to ourselves people and experiences that will confirm these negative perceptions, which are in fact unconscious affirmations. And our health will be negatively affected as a result.

The trick is to convert the energy we conduct through our body/minds from negative to positive. This will have a significant impact on our mental/emotional health and our spiritual state as well. The following exercise offers a way to discover those negative experiences and emotions trapped in our bodies and replace them with new and positive emotions, experiences, or images. This exercise will awaken the imaginative child in you. Be willing and open to take this body tour.

PRACTICE: THE BODY TOUR

Sit or lie down in a comfortable place where you will not be disturbed. It is best to do this practice in dim light or in the dark, not in a brightly lit area. Take several total breaths and use the autogenic, or deep relaxation, method to bring yourself into the intuitive Mindshift state. (Counting backward from 20 or 10 to 0 while feeling the body grow heavier and more relaxed is always an effective method.)

Now prepare to go into and explore any or all body areas, or whichever draws your attention—head, throat, chest, back, belly, groin, arms, hands, buttocks, legs, feet. As you put your attention in each area, relax, feel, and explore; allow that area to communicate to you in any way and be sensitive to any message or signal that may appear to you.

You may see an image, feel an emotion, or even discover a story hidden in this physical place. Suppose you put your attention into your heart and feel a sense of tightness, heaviness, or weight. Notice how any sensation is almost immediately associated with a word or concept in your mind. First comes the sensation, then the description: "tightness, heaviness, weight." You may also see a corresponding image, such as a clenched fist, a gnarled root, a stone. Intuitively explore this feeling or image and see what scene arises out of this.

Perhaps you recall an unresolved relationship with your mother or former husband or wife that still weighs on your heart. What scenes from this painful relationship come to mind? What unresolved issues are still weighing on your heart? Were you betrayed or did you betray? Was there some misunderstanding? Are you still holding on to anger, sadness, bitterness? Notice any negative or painful feelings you may have regarding this situation. Explore these until the feelings or issues become clear. Record your explorations here.

_____

_____

_____

Now, from your heart, affirm with feeling whatever statement addresses this unresolved issue. If you need to apologize, forgive, bless, release, or all of the above, feel the heaviness or tightness in your heart and affirm this almost like a prayer. Do this for at least one minute and notice any change of sensation in that area. This affirmation or prayer is a conscious replacement of negative or disturbing thoughts with healing feelings, thoughts, and energy.

Now see this person or situation in a new light. See him or her and yourself at a time when you were both happy. Bless both him or her and yourself by holding in your heart that image of mutual happiness, and leaving it there. Blessing is wishing another person to be whole, knowing that wholeness heals the world in both tangible and mysterious ways. Blessing releases painful emotions that trap energy, toxify the body, and contribute to illness. Blessing is spiritual Qi Gong.

My experience with this practice was _____

_____

_____

Another method you can use with this practice is to let the organ or part of your body you are exploring on this tour tell a story. Perhaps you are paying attention to your stomach, which often suffers from acids, problems with digestion, or even an ulcer. You may notice feelings such as anxiety or loneliness, but no clear image or person appears. Go with that feeling and create a scene using whatever image the feeling brings to mind. Perhaps you see a frightened child walking alone through a dark, eerie forest.

Whatever scene appears, turn it into a story. Tell why the child is there and what he or she is doing or searching for. Let the story flow freely. The image or scene that comes will likely be analogous to the feelings trapped in that part of your body. By making these feelings conscious, you can rewrite the story. Perhaps the lost, frightened child in the dark forest meets a wise old magician or a fairy queen who blesses him or her and gives him or her an object of power—a magic sword that gives its user strength and courage or a large, luminous jewel whose radiance heals all wounds, banishes evil, and lights the way out of the forest.

Feel every aspect of this story as you shift it from darkness to light and woundedness to wholeness. Be the author of your own healing story, and install its healing power in any area of your body that you may be working on.

Now explore several more areas of your body, using whichever of these methods feels appropriate. Use the images, stories, affirmations, and prayers that come to you in relation to these old wounds any time you feel the need for further healing. Your response to what you are discovering in each area can be recorded on a tape or in writing.

When you have finished your tour of the body, note which areas have an uncomfortable feeling attached to them. Go back to any of these areas. Let your guide ask you to recall a time when you felt particularly good. As those pleasant memories come up, let them be transferred to the troubled area.

Record what you experienced in each bodily area:

Head _____

_____

_____

Chest _____

_____

_____

Back _____

_____

_____

Shoulders _____

_____

_____

Arms _____
_____
_____

Stomach _____
_____
_____

Buttocks _____
_____
_____

Legs _____
_____
_____

Feet _____
_____
_____

What areas felt particularly uncomfortable? _____
_____
_____

What memories did you retrieve when you felt particularly good? _____
_____
_____
_____
_____
_____
_____

How do you feel after transferring the positive memories to the area filled with discomfort? _____

_____

_____

_____

_____

_____

FORGIVENESS HEALS

Asking for Forgiveness

Forgiveness is one of the most powerful measures for health and is essential for aligning the body, mind, heart, and soul. The following exercise, one inspired by Sheba, will take you beyond your imagination and into physical reality, stimulating and awakening your energies through actual personal encounters. The intent is to locate and help heal any wound or injury you may have caused another person by your words or actions. While this exercise can be done at any time, it is particularly appropriate at the beginning of a new year, when you are reflecting on your actions of the past year.

———————— ☀ ————————

PRACTICE: MAKING AMENDS

Go to any of the people in your life whom you may have intentionally or unintentionally injured in some way, either physically or emotionally. If you know what you did, proceed directly to the apology. If you really do not know, then ask sincerely, "Is there anything that I have done this past year that may have hurt, injured, or upset you? If there is, I want to make it right." Listen as the other person tells you what you have done. Then look him or her in the eye and say, "I'm sorry," and take action to make amends. If the person you are trying to get to forgive you is surprised or taken aback by this request, you can once again express your sincerity and add, "I want to release and heal any resentment that has been caused by me this past year or at any other time. I sincerely want to know if any of the people who have been in my life have been hurt by me." When the person shares his or her grievances in response, don't argue or speak defensively. Simply say, "I'm really sorry. That was not my intention. What can I do to make it better?"

Sometimes unreasonable demands arise in response to these queries. If you are presented with an unreasonable request, you can say, "I can't do that, but I can do this. I can do part of it." Then do what you can.

Once you have asked for forgiveness and have dealt with anything you need to correct, then the most important thing of all is to forgive yourself. You are, after all, a human being.

Also, sometimes it is not possible to do this face-to-face. The other person may have died, have moved away, or be unwilling to speak with you. If so, perform this as an inner practice using the Mindshift Method. You should, however, perform face-to-face with at least one person.

List the people to whom you owe amends. _____

_____

_____

_____

What insights or emotions came out of this practice? _____

_____

_____

_____

What type of release did you feel after doing this practice? _____

_____

_____

_____

Were some encounters more difficult than others? Why? _____

_____

_____

_____

_____

Asking for forgiveness requires genuine humility and a willingness to see and acknowledge the pain we may have caused others. But the truth is that we cannot truly receive forgiveness without being willing to offer it to others. Twenty years ago I heard a woman tell the story of her near-death experience. She found herself in the other world with an angelic guide, who at one point told her, "Those who refuse to forgive break the bridge that they themselves must one day cross over." It cannot be said more clearly than that.

Forgiving Others

We often hold on to the bitterness of old wounds, recalling the insults and betrayals of others as if they happened only yesterday. Meanwhile, anger boils inside us, depleting our vital energy and toxifying our body/minds. Forgiveness is the release of self-destructive emotion futilely aimed at others. It can take a thousand forms. And when it is truly accomplished, it brings an incredible peace and relief to the body/mind.

PRACTICE: IMAGERY FOR FORGIVING OTHERS

Take the time to make a list of everyone whom you feel has ever mistreated you, harmed you, or done you an injustice, or toward whom you still feel resentment, hostility, or anger. Some people may bring up feelings of rage, others only feelings of mild irritation. But they all belong on your list. (You may want to make two lists, one of heavyweights and one of lightweights.) Next to each person's name, write down what he or she did that caused you pain or incurred your wrath.

Then close your eyes, relax, and visualize yourself having a conversation with each of these people, one on one. Explain your grievance clearly and state your intention to release it as a negative force from your mind and heart, to no longer be bound to them by negative emotions for the sake of your own healing. If you can genuinely forgive this person and dissolve the anger still existing between you, do so. Imagine that you are facing this person and holding hands. Feel love flowing from your heart into this other person's heart, forming a spiritual bond with this person with whom you have shared an instructive life drama. Intuitively feel into the lesson it contained. Then see yourself stepping away from them as you affirm: "I release my hold on you and wish you well in whatever you choose to do. Thank you for releasing your hold on me and wishing me well as I go on with my life." Give them a blessing and say, "I forgive you and release you. Go your own way and be happy."

Yet it is not always possible to forgive another in this way in one sitting. Forgiveness is like weight lifting—you may have to build up your forgiveness muscles to handle some heavyweight grievances in your past. Perhaps the best you can do is to release the anger and bitterness that you know poisons you and release the other person to one better able to carry the weight, such as the Universe or God. When you have finished this process, write across the entire list "I now forgive or release you all."

Since you will be keeping this list on a separate piece of paper, you can periodically update the names of the people you want to forgive, and work with them in this way until you feel "complete."

After this practice, do you feel more relaxed, or peaceful in your relationship with these people? Record what emotions you are feeling after this release. _____

_____

_____

_____

ILLNESS, MEANING, AND TRANSFORMATION: THE BIG PICTURE

Before you begin the following practice, repeat the following affirmation several times, letting it sink into your consciousness: "All illness, injury, or crisis is a doorway to transformation." This truth gives meaning to every human ordeal. Often when we are ill, disabled, or overcome by stress, we lose sight of this big picture. We become locked into conflict as our focus narrows to "me and this disease or injury." We feel like victims of fate. The purpose of this practice is to shift your perspective to "What is the possibility that lies beyond this illness? What is at stake for me in this?"

PRACTICE: GETTING THE BIG PICTURE

Perform this practice in your Mindshift area where you will not be disturbed. Sit comfortably or lie down, take several total breaths, and enter the Mindshift state through conscious relaxation, which should be fairly simple for you to do by now.

Now, examine your life and locate a dilemma or an unresolved situation that your ailment might represent. Are you staying in a job that makes you miserable because you're afraid you can't survive without it? Are you staying in a bad relationship for similar reasons? Are you not following your heart in some significant area? Are you the person you want to be, living the life you want to live? What issue or circumstance comes to mind that seems in some way connected to the condition or situation you are trying to heal? _____

_____

_____

Let us use Robert as an example. Robert has been having migraine headaches for several years, and the doctor can find no physiological cause. But using this practice, Robert realizes that he has been in the same dead-end office job for ten years now; this leaves him in a constant state of low-grade despair. He sees that he is staying there out of fear that he won't be able to find a job that will pay as much. He would really like to complete the psychology degree he abandoned years ago when his wife got pregnant and he had to quit school to support his family. He longs to work directly with people in the service field. But he will have to go to night school for three years to complete his degree, and he's been procrastinating for years now, thinking he's just too tired after work and school would take him away from his family more than he would like.

Robert sees that by staying in his job and giving up on his dream he is unconsciously choosing this constant state of despair and fear in which he feels trapped. He sees that this is not only exhausting him but also making him sick.

Robert's story is a good model of this connection between our ailments and the ruts in which we may have gotten stuck. You must see and feel the connection between your state of health and the life you are presently living. Remember, if the life you are living is making you unhappy, it is also undermining your health in innumerable ways.

Having realized the connection between your ailment and a corresponding life issue, you can see your condition in a new context. You are no longer a victim of fate. You are a person in a challenging situation who can now by concrete actions change your fate and restore your health. This new perspective gives meaning to your illness. And it gives you powerful motivation and a new way to address the fundamental life issue that underlies it. Addressing this issue becomes a process of healing, of becoming whole. Your illness is now an opportunity for transformation.

The next step is to make a concrete plan and commit to it wholeheartedly, as if your life depended on it. The fact is that your life very well may. A sense of urgency gives you motivation and power. When you hold your illness in the context of this new goal, you have something at stake—your own healing and transformation. No longer a victim of fate, you are now the hero of your own myth, on a quest for your goal, with very real dragons to fight—your own doubts and fears.

Once you take on as a challenge a situation to which you have previously surrendered, a shift in your energy occurs. This shift and this energy are signs of real healing and transformation. Wage a campaign like a soldier in battle fighting for his or her life. And every step you take toward your goal will make you a new, stronger, and healthier person.

Having done this practice, write down the results.

The unresolved issue or circumstance connected to my ailment is _____

_____

_____

The action I plan to take to resolve this situation is _____

_____

_____

Chapter Ten

_____

CALLING THE HOTLINE FOR
ANOTHER PERSON

When a dear friend or loved one is ill or injured, a common
tendency is to kiss the sore spot to make the pain go away.
Yet do we ever pause to ask ourselves "Does the person really want
to be healed?" Should we enter another's bodily house uninvited,
unaware of the issues involved? Even when another consents to our
healing intent, we still need to understand the mental, emotional,
and spiritual dynamics underlying an ailment before any healing can
be completely effective. This chapter examines the intricacies involved in extending a healing hand and presents a new application
of the Mindshift Method to help another gain insight into his or her
malady. You will also learn how to direct healing energies to a person
whether physically present or at a distance.

EXTENDING A HEALING HAND

We have by now established that despite a wide variety of surface
or physical causes of health ailments, potent mental, emotional, and
spiritual dynamics often underlie a dis-ease or illness. For example,
the subconscious may create minor symptoms that force a person to
rest in order to avoid a more serious health crisis later on. Or an
accident suddenly occurs, incapacitating the person so the needed

rest and repair can finally take place. The plot thickens when you, the healer, enter the picture to restore this person to wholeness. Will you take away the excuse for not writing the annual report, giving a dreaded speech, confronting a family member? Perhaps the illness is a subconscious retreat from obligations or demands that the person is not prepared to meet. Yet here you are, extending a healing hand—threatening to thrust the ailing one right back into a situation he or she is trying to avoid. And when your healing efforts fail, you ask, "Why isn't the healing working?"

Unlocking the Hidden Rewards of Dis-ease

Dis-ease or illness brings many secondary gains, such as forcing rest upon a depleted individual or eliciting the attention and nurturing the person may secretly crave. Illness may also give an individual the time for introspection necessary to discover the next step on life's journey. And let us not forget the symbolic messages being sent when a knee, eye, or hand, for example, is taken out of circulation. As explained earlier, every ailment is a possible doorway to transformation; every crisis may blossom into a gift of living. So can you or I rightfully march in with a healing kit?

As the following example illustrates, healing energies can't penetrate until the person is receptive, both consciously and subconsciously, to the idea of becoming whole. Recently I talked to a colleague who complained of a painful eye problem. She had discontinued her therapy after three months when the physical pain persisted. She had not yet considered that nonphysical or psychological issues might lie at the roots of her ailment. When she ignored my suggestions about the body/mind connection, I took the cue and packed up my healing kit, realizing that any attempt at healing was futile until she was truly ready to open her eyes and look beyond her physical symptoms.

Letting the Healer Enter

As a healer you can knock on a sick person's door, but you cannot enter without permission. The first step is to put all your good intentions aside and ask if calling the healing hotline for this person is appropriate. Does this individual want to heal?

My gifted friend Pete Raynolds can summon healing energies into his hands to sense energy blockages in a person's body. But Pete always asks for permission before releasing the energy flow in another person's body. I once asked him to do a healing for my husband, Jim. Pete smiled and said, "Jim has to ask me for the healing." Thus Pete reminded me that for a healer's efforts to be effective, the ailing person must make a request for healing and must be receptive on every level; he or she must want to get well. I have heard countless people say that they want to get better, yet they fail to respond to all healing efforts. All you can do when someone is not receptive to being healed is silently offer a prayer that they will respond when the time is right for them and that they may resolve the issues underlying their illness and achieve the wholeness they desire.

Admittedly, when I hear someone is ill, my first inclination is to send a healing prayer. But I stop to consider that perhaps the person has subconsciously chosen his or her illness for reasons beyond my ken. The other day a friend told me about his sore throat. When I asked if he would like me to send him healing energy he quickly said yes. Another friend had a heart problem that was more serious. I knew this problem had ramifications on many other levels, but still I *asked* if I could send healing. She said she would welcome my prayers. As her healing needs were more complex, she didn't begin to mend until five weeks later, after she realized what her heart problem symbolized. She was literally brokenhearted over people in her work environment whose insensitivity had caused her untold grief.

For this next practice, think of all the people you know who are ill or injured, with ailments from minor to serious. They can be people you know well or casually. The purpose of this exercise is to become aware of how you enter the healing space and characteristically respond. For now, simply observe your reactions and tendencies. All healers must cultivate self-awareness.

PRACTICE: OBTAINING PERMISSION TO HEAL

Become very aware of the people around you at work, in your social setting, or in your family. Some may have long-standing illnesses, chronic infirmities, or periodic temporary ailments such as colds or flus. For this practice, select one person. How did you feel or respond when you heard about this person's illness? _____

_____

_____

_____

Now you want to be a healer and help the person become whole. Ask this person if you can send healing energies in some way. How does the person respond? _____

_____

_____

If the response is positive, how do you feel about being able to augment this person's healing process? _____

_____

_____

If the person doesn't respond to your healing intent, seems ambivalent or unreceptive, speculate as to how the illness might be serving the person in light of what you know about him or her. ___

_____

_____

Is there another, more effective way you can approach this person in the future? _____

_____

_____

_____

_____

Guiding the Other Person's Healing

There is another quandary involved in attempting to heal another. Every symptom is a cry for help, signaling something amiss on the mental, emotional, and/or spiritual level. So you extend a healing hand and the physical symptom vanishes, only to reappear later as the person succumbs to illness again. For how can true healing occur if the nonphysical issues underlying the ailment have never been addressed and resolved? Analogously, a pill can temporarily ease the pain of an infected wound, but the pain will persist until the infection is cured and the wound is healed. True healing must address the origins of an illness, not merely confront the symptoms. And that healer is most effective who gives others the intuitive tools to accomplish this deeper work.

Let us now review the techniques you've learned so far that will help you facilitate another person's healing. The first step is to do a body scan and discover which part or condition needs healing. This inquiry begins at the physical level. Next you can go beneath the surface and call upon your inner physician to diagnose the symbolic meaning of this person's ailment. This insight indicates what adjustments in the psyche need to be made for a healing to occur. The third step is to access the appropriate remedy from your inner physician's healing bag that will help the other person address the cause of the physical ailment. This might entail him or her forgiving someone, resolving a negative situation, or taking active measures to rebuild sagging self-esteem. In the final step, the person can heal only when the lesson is discovered that will bring the body, mind, heart, and soul into alignment.

The following example illustrates each of these steps. Stephen wishes to do a healing for his friend Paul, who lives seven hundred miles away. He starts with the body scan. He closes his eyes, scans Paul's body for energy blockages, and notices patches of darkness around the heart. Focusing on this area, Stephen takes the second step: he elicits a symbolic image that will reveal the issue underlying Paul's condition. He sees a black heart pierced by a sword dripping blood. Paul has recently broken up with his girlfriend. He says he is fine, but this image shows he is still aching from the loss of this relationship. Stephen is concerned about Paul's health and calls to see how he is feeling. He finds out that Paul is feeling despondent because his doctor just prescribed pills to regulate his heartbeat.

This gives Stephen feedback that his intuitive diagnosis is confirmed, so he goes on to the third step: finding an appropriate tool to help Paul resolve this situation. Sheba Penner's method of filling a painful area with happier memories seems appropriate. When Stephen talks to Paul about his recent separation, he can ask Paul to remember the good moments of his relationship or a time in his life when he felt happy. Then he can teach Paul to install this positive memory in his heart.

Finally, Stephen asks his inner physician for an insight into Paul's relationship. Stephen senses that Paul invests too much in other people, putting them on pedestals. Paul becomes so involved in giving that he neglects his own needs. Stephen senses that Paul must learn to receive the same love that he gives in order to have a positive relationship. Stephen could call Paul and share this intuitive flash, but instead, he'll wait for the next time he talks to Paul. Then Stephen can ask Paul what he has learned from his recent breakup. Helping Paul figure things out for himself is more useful than giving a pat answer, which may be only part of the truth. Stephen's insight belongs to him and may not fit Paul's current situation. Stephen could apply his intuition by asking a question or two, such as "Did you idealize your girlfriend, Sue?" or "Did you put Sue up on a pedestal?" But he must not impose his insight as a cure-all. Let Paul use his own intuition to explore his issues, with Stephen's support. Note that Stephen could use imagery to send healing energy to Paul's ailing heart, just as a doctor may treat painful symptoms as well as causes. But ultimately others bear the responsibility for their own healing.

Now let's take this four-step journey to helping another person walk over the healing bridge.

PRACTICE: HELPING ANOTHER WALK OVER THE HEALING BRIDGE

Whom do you want to help across the healing bridge? _____

_____

_____

Find a time and space where you will not be disturbed for at least thirty minutes. Sit or lie comfortably and enter the Mindshift state. You can have your eyes open or closed.

First, imagine yourself entering this person's body to do a body scan. Become sensitive to any symptoms of bodily distress you find. Notice any dark or gray spots showing up on the scan. Be alerted to an area "screaming" for attention.

Second, focus on any physical area that commands your attention. Concentrating on that area, let a symbol, image, or metaphor arise to help you diagnose the condition and underlying issues, so an effective healing can occur.

Third, using the Mindshift techniques from Chapter 5, interpret the information that comes to you, and let these insights guide you in prescribing concrete measures that the person can do to heal.

Finally, what lesson is embedded in this situation, and what underlying issues must be addressed for this person to bring his or her body, mind, heart, and soul back into alignment?

When you disengage from the person, in your imagery, put him or her in a golden light, bless him or her in your own words, or give him or her an imaginary embrace.

Record your discoveries here.

What physical area or condition did you find by doing the scan?

_____

_____

_____

What symbol, image, or metaphor appeared in this area? _____

_____

_____

What Mindshift tool did you take from your inner physician bag to get insight into the image and intuit the healing path? _____

_____

_____

What lesson for the other person is embedded in this situation?

_____

_____

Write down any ideas you have on how to share your insights with this person to expedite his or her healing. _____

_____

_____

YOUR INNER PHYSICIAN—MAKING A HOUSE CALL

The following sayings illustrate two spiritual principles a true healer must embody. Mother Teresa, who was one of the most caring healers on the planet, said, "We must do small things for one another with great love." The second saying, which I use as a guide, is: "I cannot pour out happiness upon others without getting a few drops on myself." The two principles are love and interconnectedness. In the process of healing others, the healer becomes whole.

With these principles in mind, I ask you, "What small, loving thing can you do to pour happiness upon another person?" Such acts, however small, make us all healers. Love is the ultimate source of power for the healer. There is someone out there who needs your healing energies. Many people unknowingly act in a healing capacity, expecting no reward or praise, never calling themselves healers. If you consider your relationships and the way you touch the lives of the people you meet, you will become aware of the healing you already share with others. Your warm embrace, for example, can turn someone's tears into a smile. Someone who is feeling low may be uplifted by your good humor. You have helped others by being a responsive friend and a good listener. Your simple attention and concern, your smile, and your thoughtful gestures heal others more than you know. Yet you may not call yourself a healer. You magnify your healing gifts by being more aware of your healing actions and putting more of yourself into these simple gestures. As a healer, you can also pass on the tools you are learning from this book. Acknowledge friends, family members, or colleagues for their own healing gifts, and empower them to help others in turn.

Even strangers heal. When I lived in Nassau, Bahamas, during a particularly low period in my life, I frequently felt blue and confused about my future direction in life. One day I heard a loud knock at the door. When I opened it, I was surprised to see the gardener standing there holding a beautiful flower. He gave it to me, saying, "I wanted you to have this flower." With this simple gesture of caring, the light came pouring into the room and chased my blues away.

We usually confine the giving of gifts to holidays, birthdays, or special events. Yet moments of giving that are not related to a special event are invaluable. Many people who have had near-death experiences and have watched their lives pass before their eyes have said that the important acts were often the simple human gestures of kindness, generosity, concern, and affection, which they made to others in need. Now let's explore the grab bag of simple, powerful healing gifts you can give to anyone at any time to make a difference in their lives.

PRACTICE: GIVING A HEALING GIFT

In the last exercise, you thought of people you knew who were ill. In this exercise, you will be giving gifts to five of these people. Of course you can give more gifts if you want. As a healer, you can give someone in need the gift of your smile, of kindness or comfort, or of a silent blessing. Let me remind you that someone now needs your strength, helping hand, prayers, uplifting word, forgiveness, praise, encouragement, faith, love, telephone call, visit, letter, or companionship.

First, list the people in need of healing and the gifts you are giving. For each person, commit to five specific actions that involve you giving them focused, blessing energy. At least two of these gifts of healing should involve direct personal contact.

Person in Need of Healing _____ Gift _____

_____

_____

_____

_____

_____

How did you feel about giving these gifts? _____

_____

_____

_____

How do you now feel about bearing the title of healer? _____

_____

_____

_____

A Group Experience in Healing

The essential attitude of a true healer is one of love and reverence for all life. A true healer encourages others to be aware of their natural strengths and abilities. These positive attributes are easily canceled out by overly self-critical attitudes. You must assess your flaws and limitations realistically in order to rise above them, but an onslaught of self-criticism does no one any good. Such negative affirmations as "I am weak, lazy, stupid, ugly, fat, etc." magnify negativity and undermine self-esteem, and by blinding us to our natural gifts, talents, and special abilities, become self-fulfilling prophecies.

As you engage in the following group technique, notice how healing occurs when individuals transmit positive energy to others through presence, words, and actions. This practice is often done sitting in a circle with four or more people who have never met. Each member takes a turn receiving as the others, one by one, gives him or her positive energy through looks or empowering words or actions. The group is guided by two rules. The first rule is that all speech must be sincere, positive, and uplifting. Group members acknowledge one another's positive attributes and strengths without any buts. The second rule is to allow whatever surfaces to come up without judging or negating one's own responses and experience.

This practice does not have to be done with a group of strangers; a group of friends or family members will do. For those of you reading this now who do not have access to such a group, you can do this practice with one good friend or with your lover or spouse. If necessary, you can do it with yourself in the mirror. You can even do it with a pet and feel the real power of it. (Almost no one can look at you with the nonjudgmental, unquestioning love of a beloved animal friend. This accounts, no doubt, for the studies showing that people with pets live longer and stay healthier than people with none.)

The key in this practice is to make direct eye contact and to allow your words and presence to permeate the others, so they not only feel but believe your acknowledgment of them. After this practice you will notice a bright, warm, and loving atmosphere in the room, and even see it in the eyes of the other members of the group. And you will feel a new and positive energy.

It is unbelievably healing to have another person stand before you, look you in the eye, and tell you, "You are such a kind person. It shows in your face." Or "You're such a cheerful person. I love to hear the sound of your laughter." Or even "There's something about you that always makes me feel good. I love just being around you." We are so used to withholding such feelings from others that often we don't know how much people appreciate us. And by withholding our positive feelings from others, we rob them of the healing power of our admiration, appreciation, and praise.

This practice can become a daily habit. You can do it wherever you go. By paying small, sincere compliments or praising the good we see in others, even in the strangers we meet, we shower others with healing energy by reminding them of their inherent worth. And we heal and uplift ourselves. We cannot give love without experiencing love, and love heals.

Doing this daily practice will teach you to notice the good in others that gives you joy, rather than looking for faults that annoy and irritate you. The truth is that you will find what you are looking for in others and in yourself. So why not look for gold? Seeing good in yourself and others revitalizes you, while focusing on flaws is disturbing, debilitating, and unhealthy.

Become the Healing Stranger on a secret mission, a spiritual Johnny Appleseed sowing healing light and positive vibrations wherever you go. Charge your world and everyone in it with joyous energy. Smile and acknowledge the people you meet. Encourage your fellow workers and express your pleasure in their company. For one whole day don't take anyone you know or meet for granted. And at the end of the day, notice how you feel.

Now imagine if you made this practice the habit of a lifetime. The dramatic shift in your energy and health that would result would astonish you and the people who know you. You would become a walking power generator, recharging others and being recharged in turn, upping the voltage wherever you went. With this in mind, perform the following practice with at least one partner.

Begin by facing each other, making eye contact. Consciously relax your body and be fully present with this person. Remember, the eyes are the window to the soul. See the soul looking out at you from that window and feel the mystery of this. Now tell your partner one admirable trait you have always seen, admired, or loved in him or her. Relay how this person is courageous, inspiring, or insightful. Fully express your impression of him or her by illustrating it with an image or scenario. For example, if you see your partner as courageous, describe how you see he or she would jump in the water to rescue a drowning person or would pull a child out of a burning building. Make it graphically clear how you see your partner so he or she can see himself or herself through your eyes.

When you are finished, let your partner take his or her turn. Record your experience. _____

_____

_____

_____

_____

The Healing Whisper

The healing whisper is another variation on this practice. The power of the whisper is ancient and legendary. In mystical cults, initiation is often given through a whisper. A whisper is intimately and directly transmitted from mouth to ear into the soul of the listener. The whisper imbues one's communication with mysterious significance. Use it in this next practice and feel its power. And consciously let the messages whispered into your ears be planted deep in your mind, like healing seeds.

This practice is ideally done with a group of several people. But it is effective even if done with a single partner. Everyone first thinks of a positive message they would like to hear about themselves. It may be "You are so inspiring," "You are so beautiful," or "You radiate love." The group is then divided into receivers and senders. The receivers stand with eyes closed and wait to hear the message. The senders then go around to each person in turn and whisper the phrase they themselves would like to hear into the receiver's ear. If ten people are in the group, each receiver will hear five exquisite messages. If you are doing this with a partner instead of a group, let each partner whisper at least three empowering messages. Also, whisper in both the person's ears; let the person hear himself or herself praised in stereo.

PRACTICE: THE HEALING WHISPER

Record how you felt hearing all these wonderful messages whispered in your ears. _____

_____

_____

_____

_____

_____

The Intuitive Bond

You met Dr. Henry Reed in Chapter 4 when I described his dream helper ceremony. He is a professor of transpersonal studies at Atlantic University in Virginia Beach and the author of *Exercise Your Intuitive Heart*. Henry uses a technique called the intuitive heart discovery process to develop an intuitive healing bond with another. The main thrust of this method is to use intuition to access a past experience that might have relevance to another person's unexpressed need.

The specific ritual that evolved from the intuitive heart discovery is called "In My Own Experience." Participants in the ritual will discover how their intuition guides them to a healing story from their own experience that deeply touches someone in need of help. According to Henry, here's how it works: "While focusing on a heart connection with another person, who is silently pondering a private concern, allow yourself to come up with a memory from your own past. Describe the memory aloud and then improvise *what you have learned* from that experience."[1]

Henry recalls being paired in a workshop with a woman he didn't know. As directed, she wrote her concern on a piece of paper that no one else saw. After opening receptively to her, Henry shared a memory of himself as a teenager mowing the lawn. His mother was relaxing on the patio. When Henry missed a patch of grass, he went back to cut it and looked up to see if his mother had noticed his error. Henry intuitively linked this memory to his need for his mother's approval and his fear of her criticism. But a higher perspective showed him that he wanted to please her so she would be happy and nurture him in return. He realized that the themes attached to this memory also defined his relationships with others.

After Henry had shared all this with his partner, she told him that her question had focused on whether therapy would benefit her relationship with her mother. Henry's partner then realized that her own son's disturbing behavior with her paralleled herself in her relationship with her own mother. She responded strongly when Henry used the word "approval" and mentioned his effort to improve his mother's disposition by pleasing her. This insight was crucial for her in her situation with her son, giving her a new and healing perspective to apply in her painful family dilemmas.

Now find a partner to try this practice with.

PRACTICE: SHARING A HEALING STORY

To begin, face your partner and establish a heart connection with this person by imagining an energy field enveloping you and a radiant beam of light directly connecting you, bridging your hearts together. Let your partner quietly contemplate a troublesome issue and then write this concern down on a piece of paper. As this is happening, let your intuitive mind present you with a memory from your own past. If you wish, you can jot this recollection down on paper. Then describe the memory to your partner and share what you have learned from that experience. It is now your partner's turn to tell you his or her issue and share whatever insight your memory has provided relating to his or her concern. Then reverse roles and let your partner's intuition offer a story and insight to you as you consider your own issue. What is your partner's issue? _____

_____

_____

Calling the Hotline for Another Person

What is your memory? _____

_____

_____

_____

What did you learn from the memory? _____

_____

_____

_____

How does this insight help your partner's healing process? _____

_____

_____

_____

_____

What is your issue? _____

_____

What is your partner's memory? _____

_____

_____

_____

What did your partner learn from his or her memory? _____

_____

_____

_____

_____

How does this insight help your healing process? _____

_____

_____

_____

_____

THE HEALING POWER OF PRAYER

Prayer is a powerful and effective healing tool, whether your patient is right beside you or thousands of miles away. The outer physician most responsible for publicizing the link between prayer and healing is Dr. Larry Dossey. While prayer has been curiously overlooked by most of the medical profession, Dr. Dossey has gathered a large body of research, much of which was virtually buried by a medical establishment made uncomfortable by its spiritual and metaphysical implications. According to Dr. Dossey, prayer is much more than bowing your head with your hands clasped. It includes an attitude of prayerfulness and feelings of love, compassion, and empathy directed toward another person.

In his book *Healing Words: The Power of Prayer and the Practice of Medicine*, Dr. Dossey reviews the results of 130 experiments where prayer as a healing modality was tested in the laboratory.[2] He shows how the dramatic and powerful workings of the mind through prayer can effect healing. For example, in a 1988 study of coronary care patients in San Francisco, California, one group was prayed for by the research staff and one was not. This was a classic double-blind study where neither the patients nor the hospital staff knew who was being prayed for. Only the researchers knew! Thus the hospital staff was prevented from inadvertently giving special treatment to one group or the other. After ten months, the prayed-for group was significantly healthier than the non-prayed-for group. This group was five times less likely to require antibiotics and three times less likely to develop a condition where the lungs fill with fluid. Also, none of the prayed-for group required an artificial airway in the throat, while twelve in the non-prayed-for group did.[3]

I am always amazed when I and others pray for a person at a distance and see undeniable results of healing occur. Dr. Dossey is also still mystified by the nonlocal nature of prayer, where healing energies induced by prayer occur unlimited by space and time. For example, the prayers of a friend who lives in a distant locale, even at the other side of the world, can be highly effective. The idea that your mind reaches beyond your body and its immediate surroundings is validated every time someone effects a healing from a distance or makes a long-range intuitive diagnosis without recourse to medical technology. Both experiences come under the "nonlocal mind" rubric and are described by Dr. Dossey in detail.

There are, of course, as many kinds of prayer as there are individuals. Prayer can simply refer to becoming still and communing with your inner physician, your higher self, your guardian angel, your beloved friend, the Tao, the universal mind, or God. Who knows, perhaps they are all the same. For prayer is equally effective whatever method is used. In fact, most of the practices in this book could be forms of prayer.

The following story illustrates the miraculous power of prayer. When I lived in Nassau, Bahamas, weekly fashion shows were one of the major attractions in the hotels. Lorenzo, a tall, handsome, well-built man who radiated joy and vitality, was one of the most popular models on the island. When Lorenzo became completely incapacitated with an undiagnosed malady, the news rapidly spread around the island. Within weeks, his languid, peaked body was unrecognizable. His rapid physical deterioration shocked everyone. Finally he lay comatose in the hospital; the doctors said he was dying. A red alert went out through every media source on the island, asking people to pray at a specified time for Lorenzo. Days later he began to respond. Miraculously, the whole island watched him return from the brink of death and regain his strength and vitality. Whenever I return to the island and see the broad grin on Lorenzo's handsome face, I rejoice at this living testimony to the power of prayer.

Of course, you can pray by yourself for friends or family members who need your help. But the power of prayer is multiplied when others join you. United, the individual thoughts and prayers become a mighty river of healing. I imagine an orchestra before the concert begins and the discordant sounds of everyone tuning individual instruments. But when the conductor's baton signals, the players unite and the result is a harmonious and powerful blending of notes called a symphony. This is what happens when we unite in prayer. The person for whom we are praying receives a spiritual symphony of immeasurable healing power.

Remember that no one can tell you exactly how to pray. Choose the method that meets your individual needs. You can pray in silent contemplation or enthusiastically, speaking your words out loud. The power of prayer is effective whether offered while driving down

the highway, standing in the shower, or kneeling in a church, syna-
gogue, or temple.

PRACTICE: THE POWER OF PRAYER

Let's return again to "Giving a Healing Gift" (page 175), where you
listed five people who needed healing. Pick one of them now and
send a healing prayer during the same time period each day for one
week. At the end of the week, inquire about your friend's health.
See if he or she has noticed any change or improvement. You might
ask your friend if day or time seem significant in the healing process.
(Remember, it is important to pick a person who seems receptive to
you and your healing intentions.)

How did you feel when you engaged in prayer? _____

_____

_____

_____

What results did you find at the end of a week? _____

_____

_____

_____

_____

_____

Also, see if you can gather or join a prayer group to perform the
same practice above.

The Prayer of Light

Let's end this chapter with a beautiful prayer of light that came
through Dr. Patrick Tribble, a chiropractor from Berkeley, California, who uses his intuitive abilities in his healing practice with his
clients.

> At this time, I ask that the Golden Light enter your body,
> from the top of your head to the tips of your toes, going
> through every cell in your body, cleansing, purifying, and neu-
> tralizing anything that is negative. I ask that the light cleanse,

purify, and revitalize your body, giving whatever is needed at this time. May this light bring in the golden light of knowledge, wisdom, and healing. We ask that this light be neither too much nor too little. As this light enters your body we ask that each one of the four bodies be surrounded in the golden light. We ask that the physical, mental, emotional, and spiritual bodies all be in perfect alignment. May the light be used for the benefit of the highest good of yourself and the highest good of those around you.

Chapter Eleven

MINIMIZING DEBILITATING STRESS: A HEALTHY BODY, MIND, HEART, AND SOUL

AN INTRODUCTION TO MANAGING STRESS

M anaging stress and putting it to work for you is the central theme of this chapter. The members of your internal governing board—body, mind, heart, and soul—have much to teach you about managing stress, whether physical, mental, emotional, or spiritual. For stress occurs at every level of the being. And if it is not processed at every level, it will negatively affect your health.

You can't always change your environment, but you can change the way you perceive, react, and adapt to stressful situations. Difficulties can be viewed as disasters or challenges, and we can view ourselves as victims or heroes in our own drama. The Chinese word for crisis is *weiji*, which combines two characters that separately mean "danger" and "opportunity." Every problem encountered in life has these two sides. Without the element of danger, risk, or stress, there is no real opportunity for growth. To a hero, a crisis forces us to call on untapped resources and cultivate new skills that transform us, making us wiser, stronger, and more alive than before. It is truly said that strength and character are forged on an anvil, not in an easy chair.

Perspective is everything. Fear and excitement produce nearly identical effects in our bodies. Only one negatively impacts our health, while the other affects us positively. Another example of the power of perspective is that of certain Indian yogis famous for handling snakes and befriending wild tigers; these men would certainly be bitten or devoured if they had not mastered the art of shifting their perspective, which alters the behavior of these dangerous creatures. You too can learn to view irritating or difficult people differently, changing the context in which you relate to them and shifting the relationship onto new ground. The overBEARing supervisor might be imagined as a cuddly, approachable teddy bear, or you might imagine yourself as a fearless bear hunter, standing your ground, stalking your next trophy.

An important axiom of modern psychology is that without stress you would have no need to learn, change, or grow. Events need not be catastrophic to produce stress. The fact is that life's daily demands are inherently stressful—changing life patterns, promotions, firings, accidents, arguments, driving, deadlines, hectic schedules, and the basic lack of predictability or control in your life. All these create emotional stress—anxiety, fear, uncertainty, frustration, or anger—which produces physiological correlates from shallow breathing, a rapid heartbeat, headaches, and high blood pressure to ulcers and even strokes and heart attacks.

All experience has a direct impact on your body/mind in some way. Yet you can learn to interpret and use your experience in a way that reduces its negative impact and enhances its positive impact. As you learned in Chapter 6, proactive measures are the best defense against stress-related health ailments. Breathing, relaxation, centering, and imagery or meditation techniques all strengthen your body/mind and release accumulated stress.

Stress management requires willpower and an active commitment to health and happiness. The all-too-common crisis management approach to health—the rushed treatment of a full-blown stress-related ailment—is the least effective. So learn to listen to your body/mind's subtle warning signals, under the guidance of your inner physician, and regenerate radiant health as a daily habit.

MANAGING STRESS

Your body/mind always knows when you are stressed. And it tells you exactly what you need, exactly when you need it. You can access subtle levels of information—consciously tune into physical, mental, and emotional cues—and learn to identify your unique indicators of stress. By listening to the signals sent to you by your body, mind, and feelings, you can locate sources of stress early and address and release their effects *before* they injure and debilitate. The following example illustrates one way to do just this.

Your Body Knows

Joan, a saleswoman, crisscrosses the country each week to sell her product to various buyers. She often feels shaky while waiting in the boarding area of the airport, especially on weekends, when the airport is the most crowded. Her sensitive body seems to absorb the agitation of the people around her. For years Joan reacted to this stress by nervously eating airport junk food washed down with coffee, which did little to calm her nerves. But now Joan has learned to shield herself in this anxiety-inducing atmosphere by using the following imagery technique.

As soon as she arrives in the boarding area, she sits down, eyes closed, and briefly enters the intuitive relaxation state. Then she imagines herself stepping into a garment bag filled with protective white light and zipping it up. From inside, she sees and feels the light permeate her body, charging her cells with protective healing energy. Then she boards the plane, energized and oblivious to her formerly unsettling surroundings. (She also uses this technique before her sales meetings; only in these situations she emerges from her garment bag to meet her clients clothed in radiant white light.)

The first key to addressing stress is becoming aware of it. Usually we tend to ignore it, but we are better off noticing and acknowledging it. We can then consciously put our attention on what heals.

Freeway traffic is a contemporary stress zone for millions of Americans. The widespread phenomenon of road rage demonstrates what can happen when stress builds up to the breaking point. Richard, a very gentle and considerate person who commutes daily to work, noticed that every time he was in traffic, his heart began to race, his breathing grew shallow, and he became impatient and hostile. Realizing he was being absorbed into the mass psyche of commuter traffic, Richard consciously declared his car to be his temple on wheels. He began each morning's commute with a prayer for inner peace and then spent the first fifteen minutes in the car chanting centering affirmations and blessing the other drivers. His driving personality immediately changed, he began to enjoy his new freeway meditation time, and he found that his entire day benefited noticeably from the effects of this healing morning ritual. Richard transformed a formerly stressful activity into a daily healing ritual.

PRACTICE: CONFRONTING STRESS HEAD-ON

Now consider how you might apply Joan's or Richard's approach to a stressful circumstance in your life. Find a frequently recurring situation that tends to make you nervous, irritable, or upset. The next time you approach this circumstance, prepare in advance using one or more of the proactive Mindshift Methods—breathing, relaxation, centering, imagery—and note any shifts in your perspective and experience that occur. Then use this ritual daily for one week, again noting the results.

The recurring stressful situation is _____

_____

_____

The method I applied was _____

_____

_____

The shifts I noticed were _____

_____

_____

The following Mindshift Method can be applied to stress-related ailments such as heart palpitations, high blood pressure, and even anxiety attacks or simple impatience. The next time you experience one of these modern maladies, stop, relax, and imagine a metronome or timer inside your chest. Notice how fast it is swinging or ticking, and feel and see it slowing down. Think, "Slower . . . slower . . . slower . . ." and notice what happens.

You can creatively apply the Mindshift imagery method to any physical ailment, and shift any mental, emotional, or spiritual state. Enter the Mindshift state and ask for the appropriate healing image or technique so your inner physician can promptly supply the perfect remedy.

For instance, Melissa called on her inner physician, seeking a remedy for the tightness in her chest. The image that came to her was a logjam. She realized this was how she felt—as if she had a logjam inside her chest. Then she imagined Paul Bunyan, the mythical American logger, coming out of the forest, wading into the river, and one by one, pulling the logs out in his giant hands and sending them floating downstream until the river, and her chest, was open and flowing again. Since then, Joan has used this very effective visualization whenever she feels tightness in her chest.

A stressed-out person feeling all tied up in knots can mentally untangle a knotted ball of twine. And if the ball is too knotted, that person can use Alexander the Great's approach and sever it with the single stroke of a sword, for that sudden feeling of release. A person with tense shoulders can visualize barbells being removed from his or her shoulders. Or for an epic feeling of relief, a person can see himself as Atlas, with the earth on his shoulders, standing up straight and letting it roll off into space. Who needs to carry a world of problems on his back anyway?

The great Indian sage Ramana Maharshi recommended a wonderful imagery technique to provide spiritual relief for any burdened soul. He said that we are all in the hands of the Divine Power, like passengers riding on a train. And when we ride on an ordinary train, we do not continue to stand, carrying our luggage. We set it down and relax, knowing it is being carried for us. In the same way, whenever we feel burdened by our baggage in life, we can realize this, and simply set our burdens down, knowing we can rest and let God's train carry our burdens.

Visualizing what your stress looks like sparks your creativity and can provide perfect intuitive remedies. I often picture the stress or tension in my body as a kink in a garden hose. Whether your stomach is knotted before giving a public presentation or you are suffering from constipation, seeing a twisted garden hose in the ailing area slowly untwisting and feeling the water flow can produce marvelous and very practical results. Pick a physical symptom of tension that you experience periodically or chronically, and apply one of the above imaging techniques, or discover a new one with the help of your internal physician.

PRACTICE: PICTURING THE PAIN

List a recurring physical symptom that plagues you. _____

_____

_____

_____

Devise or choose an image or visual metaphor to help you ameliorate the symptom when it next appears. Record this image here.

_____

_____

_____

The Breath of Life

An important reminder: Don't take your breathing for granted! Ninety percent of your energy potentially comes from your breathing. Yet most people typically use only 10 percent of their breathing capacity. Shallow breathing leaves you cranky, tired, and stressed out. Total breathing rejuvenates and regenerates! Engage life through your breath, for breath *is* life!

Stop randomly through the day to notice your breath. Are you relaxed and breathing deeply? Notice how any tense situation inhibits your breathing. Notice how constrained breathing inhibits your participation in life at this moment. Now breathe deeply and participate more fully in life. Set your watch to beep every hour on the hour, and make that your "breath is life" check-in time.

The following practice, the "Ha!" breath, is a dynamic way to recharge your body/mind with energy. It is like switching on your force field, and like the shout of the martial artist before delivering a strike, it generates a burst of Qi, or life force, and is better than a lunch-hour cocktail. You may want to do it at home or in your car on your lunch break, as it is apt to raise eyebrows, as well as the energy, in the office.

PRACTICE: EXPERIENCE THE "HA!" BREATH

The most effective posture for this breath is either standing or sitting upright. It helps to place your hands on your stomach just above the waist with your fingertips meeting near your navel.

Begin the practice by inhaling and inflating an imaginary balloon in your belly. Then exhale with an explosion of air and shout, "Ha!" When first practicing this breath, you can push your stomach in with your fingertips as you exhale. Repeat this sequence five to seven times.

Now close your eyes and observe how you feel in mind and body. Write down any observations from your experience. For example, you may feel a warm tingling in the center of your body or an electric, energized state. This is common when the deep stress is released from the pit of your stomach. Many people feel like laughing while they are doing the "Ha!" breath, and some do break into spontaneous laughter. And you know laughter is the best medicine.

How does your body feel after the "Ha!" breath? _____

_____

How does your energy level feel? _____

_____

How does your mind feel? _____

_____

How do you feel emotionally? _____

_____

_____

_____

MENTAL TECHNIQUES TO IMAGINE
YOURSELF WELL

Our unconscious thoughts and mental pictures are incredibly potent. Our minds can create heaven or hell. And by shifting our *thoughts* and *mental processes* through imagery we can convert the negative forces of the outside world into positive internal states and produce healing transformation.

Picture yourself for a moment as the healthiest you have ever been or hoped to be. Now hold that picture (or sculpture) in your mind. Envision yourself full of energy, every cell in your body cellebrating life. In the same way you can picture yourself learning new skills or overcoming fears. These images could be called self-prophecies, for they are true pictures of the person you can become. The ancient practice of magic lay in this once secret knowledge, that what you hold in your mind alters reality to the degree of your intensity of focus. These pictures you have created are images of your birthright of radiant health and ever-expanding life. Keep them in mind!

Changing Your Inner Relationship to Outer Reality

When you feel weighed down by negative thoughts and feelings, you can use creative imagery to change your state and even influence your external environment, whether it is a chaotic home or a disturbing work environment. I use the acronym FAITH for this technique; it reminds me of my inherent power as a human being to change my inner and even outer world.

Here are the five faith-filled steps of this technique.

- *Focus on a goal.* Choose something that you truly want to do, have, or achieve. For example, "I would like to feel more calm in my work environment."
- *Affirm it as a present reality.* State your aim in a simple sentence in the present tense, as if the goal is already manifested. "I affirm this wonderful sense of inner calmness at work, no matter what pressures, distractions, or deadlines arise."
- *Imagine this state or quality is now your permanent asset.* If you

can't picture it visually, just imagine it any way you can. Embellish your picture with as many details as possible. For example, I imagine a stack of papers awaiting immediate attention piled on my desk, the phone ringing off the hook, and several people in my office asking me questions. And I see myself functioning in high gear, serenely smiling, at peace in my center.

- *Turn it over to your inner physician and let it go.* This means don't try to make it happen; just let your intuitive mind or inner physician go to work and produce the result, create the goal. For instance, when I *know* I am being guided, I can function with smooth efficiency and meet my deadlines without ending up a bundle of jangled nerves.

- *Hold the image of feeling stress free and having hearty health.* Don't question how or why this works; simply keep seeing and feeling yourself in radiant health, vibrant with the life force, no matter where you are or what you are doing or experiencing, and it will be so.

Also, notice how *meaning* and *purpose* are combined in this exercise—two factors that automatically shift our perspective and relieve stress. Having a goal or purpose gives you motivation, or energy. And when this purpose becomes the context of any life situation, it suddenly has meaning *for you*. This is the secret of the transforming power of human imagination; that it can imbue any situation, however difficult, dreadful, or even catastrophic, with purpose and meaning. By this power, which resides within each of us, hell itself can become a process of growth and transformation.

PRACTICE: USE FAITH IMAGERY

Use this creative faith imagery to focus on your health. Do you want to increase your physical fitness, lose or gain weight, increase your energy level? Do you want to heal a particular ailment?

Write your focus down in a simple, specific sentence.

My focus is to _____

_____

_____

Affirm by writing your intent in a sentence in the present tense, as if it were already true. Use phrases like "I now have" or "I am now doing."

I affirm _____

_____

_____

Imagine that your goal has come true. Close your eyes, take several deep breaths, and relax your mind and body. Repeat your affirmation several times and see it as true. "Try it on for size." See how it feels to have the desire of your focus come true. Record your images in this space, and the feelings that help you anchor your dream in your present body/mind. _____

_____

_____

_____

_____

Turn your goal over to the care of your inner physician by placing every part of the picture you have created onto an imaginary plate. Then see the plate taken and held aloft by an imaginary pair of hands.

Hold this image of letting go, feel the stress-free state, and affirm, "I turn this over to the capable hands of my inner physician, who has already helped me achieve my goal."

Record your results going through each of these steps in this space. _____

_____

_____

_____

_____

THE SPIRITUAL VIEW: SEEING THE BIG PICTURE

There is much truth in folk wisdom. Whether you see the glass as half full or half empty or a crisis as a challenging opportunity or an insurmountable obstacle can mean the difference between health and illness, courage and despair, success and failure, and even life and death. The Big Picture views the ungainly young swan as the precursor of the graceful adult swan, one of nature's most inspiring visions. It sees the mighty oak tree latent in the tiny acorn. The Big Picture expands our vision and shows the truth in such paradoxes as "Success is the end result of a series of failures" and "Our strength grows out of our wounds." The Big Picture shows every part of life in its proper place, in relation to every other part, and makes perfect sense of the whole. And our intuition calls us to that vision with a thousand daily whispers.

Intuition is a spiritual faculty whose messages originate from an inner source variously called the higher self, a higher consciousness, or the soul or spirit. Intuition has also been called the voice of God and the whispering of the Holy Spirit. And however this inner guidance comes, its wisdom can set us on the path of right actions that leads to peace of mind. Throughout this book, through the Mindshift practices, you have been working with four ancient keys that open the door to this center of spiritual knowing. They are self-observation; forgiveness and release of negativity; prayer or affirmation of the positive; and meditation on that which heals. Now for a brief review, followed by a powerful, holistic practice that incorporates these four keys and makes radiant health truly possible.

Mind and Emotion: The Doors to Heaven and Hell

In his masterpiece, *The Brothers Karamazov*, Fyodor Dostoyevsky wrote: "God and the devil are fighting, and the battlefield is the heart of man." Self-hatred, fear, guilt, anxiety, greed, resentment, anger, despair—all these and more soar like bats in the unlit cave of our heart, or subconscious mind. And as long as we allow them to, they will come and go at will, causing untold mischief.

The famous eighteenth-century philosopher and religious writer Emanuel Swedenborg said that we are all unknowingly influenced by angels and demons. These influences, he claimed, are revealed in the content of our thoughts and emotions. And it is our task to consciously choose between the angelic energy of our positive, spiritual thoughts and the demonic energy of our negative, hellish thoughts. Human beings, said Swedenborg, have the free will *in every moment* to choose whether they will live in heaven or in hell.

In her book *Fire in the Soul*, on liberating yourself from the destructive impact of negative feelings of fear, guilt, blame, and remorse, Joan Borysenko emphasizes that healing occurs when the mind peels away fear, allowing the authentic self to emerge. So perhaps much more than our health is at stake in this consideration of our thoughts and emotions.

All spiritual traditions have understood the destructive nature of negative thoughts and emotions and the healing power of positive thoughts and emotions. Thus every religion has created practices to observe and release these negative forces and cultivate or anchor one's consciousness in positive, healing energies. The basic elements of these healing practices are the four keys mentioned above—self-observation, forgiveness and release of negativity, prayer or *centering* affirmations, and meditation on what heals. These profound yet utterly simple tools enable one to notice and release toxic patterns of thought and emotion *as they arise*, then release and install in their place new patterns of thought and emotion that are healing, energizing, and life-transforming.

In these rapidly changing times, we often seem to be moving at breakneck speed into the twenty-first century, as individually and collectively we are catapulted from one storm, crisis, scandal, or challenge to another. It is in such times that we most urgently need to stop, look, and listen within, to receive healing energy and intuitive guidance from our inner physician, the still small voice of spirit within.

SPIRITUAL INTUITION AND THE FOUR KEYS
TO RADIANT HEALTH

The following four-part Mindshift practice uses the four keys of transformation to open the doorway to the intuitive wisdom and spiritual power that reside within each of us. Through attunement with this sacred space at the center, we are purified, rejuvenated, and healed at every level of our being. First we will cover each step separately, as a process in itself. Then at the end we will practice it as one four-step process.

Self-Observation: The First Step

This is the simple practice of noticing your thoughts and emotions. You can do this anywhere, anytime, under any circumstance. Engaged in randomly throughout the day, self-observation allows you to see whether your thoughts are taking you to heaven or to hell. And it will give you the clarity to choose one over the other. Since most negative thoughts and emotions occur in a state of relative unconsciousness, self-observation is a means of becoming conscious and aware of the influences arising from your subconscious mind.

Forgiveness and Release: The Second Step

Forgiveness or release is essential for true healing. The *Course in Miracles* says that "all disease comes from a state of unforgiveness. When we are ill, we need to search our hearts to see whom we have to forgive." The word "forgive" means "to give up." Forgiveness is release of that which burdens the spirit. And what burdens the spirit also afflicts the body.

Unless we consciously release the emotions inherent in our life and relationships, they remain buried in our subconscious. The acid residues of anger and unforgiveness deplete our energy and toxify our body/mind. Forgiveness of others and of ourselves, as described in Chapter 9, restores *us* to inner peace. Forgiveness does *not* mean we approve of the actions of one who has wounded or betrayed us. Forgiveness means that you release to the universe, or to God, those toxic thoughts and emotions that harm only you, and that bind you negatively to others. If you can truly bless those who have harmed you, so much the better for you. But wishing harm to another chemically harms us.

Prayer or Affirmation: The Third Step

Having observed your thoughts and emotions, and forgiven or released any negativity you may have been subconsciously meditating on, you can now *center* yourself, or anchor your mind with a prayer to your spiritual source, by whatever name you call it. You can also use a mantra or a positive affirmation such as "I open myself to the radiant life power, and feel it recharging every cell of my body and every level of my being." This third step is a conscious reprogramming of your being with positive or healing energy. It is a literal, psycho-physical repolarizing of your body/mind toward, rather than away from, the "radiant life power" that many call energy, Qi, spirit, or God.

Meditation: The Fourth Step

Having engaged the first three steps, you have now virtually entered the state of meditation. All you need to do now is remain in this calm, clear, healing state, open and receptive to the energy of spirit, which is your true nature. Let this energy fill you. Immerse yourself in it by surrendering to it. And randomly apply the first three steps as needed. This is the process of meditation. As thoughts and emotions arise, you observe them. You release them as soon as you observe them. (Or you forgive others who trouble your mind by releasing them and the emotions they stir in you.) And you center yourself in that which heals, whether you call it spirit, healing energy, or God. As you continue to meditate you will notice a sense of calmness enveloping you. Insights and inspiration may flow. Your mind may become lucid and clear. Your body may feel open, relaxed, and energized. You may also experience moments of difficulty as various disturbing thoughts and emotions arise. But you can always release them and return again to your center using this four-step process. Of course, as is true with any skill, the more you practice, the more proficient you become. And over time, this practice of observing and releasing negativity and returning to your center to meditate on the healing power within will become your natural response to the stresses of everyday living. And this, along with the other practices in this book, will change your life and bring you the radiant health you desire.

As with all the other Mindshift practices, first enter the relaxed or intuitive state. Now do these four steps and meditate for ten minutes as described above. Record your experiences when you open your eyes. _____

_____

_____

Now do this for ten minutes every morning or every evening and record your experiences each day for two weeks. _____

_____

_____

_____

_____

Become a Peace Worker

Peace Corps workers are sent all over the world to help those in need. And by meditating, you too are becoming a peace worker. You don't have to leave your home to do peace work. By meditating, you are living the words of a well-known phrase: "Let there be peace on earth, and let it begin with me." Now, when you are knocked out of your spiritual center, you know how to return. Using this simple four-step meditation practice you can regain your inner peace in the midst of a hectic day, with a ten-minute or even a ten-second meditation. Your center is only four simple steps, and perhaps only one breath, one prayer away.

And wherever you go your inner peace will affect your outer environment, and touch everyone you meet. You will naturally invoke peaceful feelings in your home, workplace, and neighborhood; in your family, friends, and coworkers. And in time, the "peace that passeth understanding" will blossom from deep within you, like the miracle of a rose unfolding.

A Peace Bulletin

I came across a piece of writing years ago. The author is unknown, and I can't even recall how it reached my hands. But the following ideas from it are a perfect way to end this section on inner peace.

SYMPTOMS OF INNER PEACE

Be on the lookout for the symptoms of inner peace. The hearts of great masses of humanity have already been exposed to inner peace and it is possible that people everywhere could become infected by this contagious condition with potentially epidemic proportions. You are hereby warned that this could pose a serious threat to what has, up until now, been a fairly stable but consistent condition of conflict in the world.

Here are some signs and symptoms of inner peace to be on the lookout for:

- A tendency to think and act spontaneously rather than on fears based on past experiences.
- An unmistakable ability to enjoy each and every moment to its fullest expression regardless of whatever others may think of it.
- A loss of interest in judging other people.
- A loss of interest in judging oneself.
- A loss of interest in interpreting the actions of others.
- A loss of interest in conflict, sarcasm, or any kind of abuse.
- A loss of the need for worry and fear (this is a very serious symptom!).
- Frequent outbursts and episodes of overwhelming ecstasy and appreciation for people and life.
- Feelings of contentment and connection with others and nature.
- Frequent attacks of smiling just for the fun of it.
- An increasing tendency to surrender to the way things are rather than forcing them to happen out of their due time.
- An increasing susceptibility to the love extended by others as well as an uncontrollable urge to share it.

• A sincere desire to make this world a better place to live because of your hope for peace, love, and prosperity for all.

WARNING!

If you have any or all of the above symptoms, please be advised that your state of inner peace may be so far advanced as not to be curable. Should you happen to be exposed to anyone else exhibiting any of these symptoms, you are advised to remain there and enjoy this dose of joy at the risk of a healthier and happier life.

PRACTICE: CHECKING YOUR SYMPTOMS

Pick at least five symptoms of peace you would like to develop. Write these symptoms down in this space. How are you feeling after a week of being exposed to them? _____

_____

_____

_____

_____

_____

Chapter Twelve

TRAVELING THE
WELLNESS TRAIL

Y ou have now charted the path that leads to wholeness and radiant
health. You have learned through the practices in this book to
enter through the Mindshift door into the intuitive realm where your
inner physician dwells. How far you travel along the wellness trail is
up to you. But I leave you with a few inspiring ideas and suggestions.

First, remember the perfect recipe for radiant health: proper food
and drink, exercise and rest, silence and stillness, humor and joy, and
a meaningful life purpose.

Your inner physician is there to guide you at every step, on all of
these levels—to help you monitor and balance your diet, physical
energy, emotional and psychological states, and even your spiritual
needs. No one can give you a set formula for living. But as you
become more and more attuned to the voice of your inner physician,
you will benefit from its constant feedback in all these areas, and its
wise guidance in the care and nurturing of your body/mind.

So eat and drink, sing and sit in silence, dance, walk and work
out, laugh and be merry—for tomorrow you live! Recharge and reflect in serenity, and follow the counsel of the physician within. Participate fully in life, knowing you will get out of life only what you
put into it. And remember that stress can either wear you down or
polish you like a fine jewel, depending on your perspective. As an
old Chinese proverb says: "The gem cannot be polished without
friction, nor man perfected without trials."

CAPTIVITY AND COCOONS

A man walking in a park discovered a partially open cocoon. Noticing movement within, he stood captivated, watching the butterfly trying to escape. Agonizing over its seemingly desperate struggle, he decided to set the butterfly free. Carefully unraveling the cocoon, he gently lifted the butterfly onto the palm of his hand and held it up toward the sky. "Fly away!" he said, elated. But the butterfly did not move. It lay dead in his hand. Its struggle to escape a cocoon it had woven about itself as a caterpillar was required to awaken the force of life within it.

Find Your Cocoon

The same struggle that gives life to the butterfly gives life to each of us. When we escape the cocoons we have often unwittingly woven about ourselves, we experience freedom. The following Mindshift Method practice will give you a new perspective on an old situation and show you a way to use it as a vehicle to greater freedom, energy, and of course, health.

PRACTICE: FINDING YOUR COCOON

Go to your Mindshift area and enter the intuitive state. Once you are there, pick a situation in your life that you view as difficult, constricting, limiting, perhaps imprisoning. Go back in time and see how it was that you first entered into this circumstance. See how at the time it fit your needs, offered you some kind of nourishment, security, benefit, or possibility of growth. What were the lessons you learned, the benefits you received, or the skills and strengths you cultivated in this situation? What purpose did it serve in your growth? See these things clearly and acknowledge them gratefully.

Now return to the present and examine the sense of confinement, limitation, or captivity you feel in this circumstance. How has this situation stopped nourishing the person you have become? Has it changed? Have you changed? Perhaps both? Does it offer further lessons and benefits that are worth staying for? Or is it no longer serving your needs; is it time to move on? Find out either what you can do to make this situation work for you or what you need to do to wrap it up and move on to the next step of your journey. See this situation as a cocoon you wove in a previous incarnation, when you were a caterpillar. Now you have devoured the nourishment it contained and grown into a new form. From this perspective, what is required for you to open your cocoon, resolve the demands of the situation, and fly free to the next level?

The situation that now feels confining is _____

_____

_____

The benefits and "nourishment" it originally offered were _____

_____

_____

The needs I now have that are not being met in this circumstance are _____

_____

_____

The steps I need to take to emerge from this cocoon and fly are

_____

_____

_____

PERSPECTIVE IS EVERYTHING

A few last words on perspective. Remember what the pessimist and the optimist have in common: neither is ever disappointed. So it is up to us to choose how we view the world, knowing our vision will be confirmed. Here are some affirmations that will help you sustain a vision of life that heals and inspires. And remember when you say the words to feel the feelings.

I let go of fear and anxiety; I let in faith and trust.
I let go of doubt; I let in confidence.
I let go of hurry; I let in poise.

I let go of hate and anger; I let in love and forgiveness.
I let go of folly and ignorance; I let in wisdom and understanding.
I let go of resentment; I let in gratitude.
I let go of darkness; I let in light.
I let go of gloom; I let in joy.
I let go of poverty; I let in prosperity.
I let go of weakness; I let in strength.
I let go of sickness; I let in health.
I let go of discord and discontent; I let in harmony and serenity.
I let go of tension; I let in relaxation.

PRACTICE: STEPS TOWARD HEALTH AND WHOLENESS

The following practice can be done using the Mindshift Method, or it can be written out in this book. Either way, it can be extremely effective in gaining a Big Picture perspective that will give you insight and motivation to make needed changes in your life.

Life/Health Assessment

First, *review your life goals* and consider the following questions:
What are your current goals? _____

_____

How do you feel about where you are and where you are going?
_____

_____

Are you on track? _____

_____

Do you feel you have the energy and motivation you need to accomplish your life goals and be the person you want to be? _____

_____

Now *review your health situation* and answer the following questions.
What is your current state of health? _____

_____

List the current negative habits that you know take their toll on your health.

Smoking? __ Overeating? __ Poor diet? __ No exercise? __ Over-working? __ Other? _____

What is the relationship between your life goals and your health issues? _____
_____
_____

Does your current state of health support or undermine your purpose? _____
_____
_____
_____

Now choose one concrete commitment you would like to make in each of the following areas: Diet. Exercise. Stillness. And Enjoyment! Make each one a simple, attainable step that you can integrate into your present life situation. Don't pick major goals to start with, like "quit smoking," or "meditate one hour a day." This practice is about initiating a process and building confidence through realistic, immediately attainable steps.

For Diet you might decide to cut down on junk food or to eat four healthy salads a week. For Exercise, you might decide to take a fifteen-minute walk four times a week or to join an aerobics or dance class. For Stillness, you might commit to beginning your day with a five-to-ten-minute serenity break using some form of meditation, visualization, or prayer. For Enjoyment, you might decide to do something you like to do once a week: go to the park, see a movie, or go out to a restaurant with a friend or your spouse or by yourself. Write your commitment in each of these four areas below.

Diet _____
_____
_____
_____
_____
_____
_____

Exercise _____

_____

_____

_____

_____

Stillness _____

_____

_____

_____

_____

Enjoyment _____

_____

_____

_____

_____

Now consider the present course of your life, the goals you now have, and the current state of your vitality and health. In the light of all this, write down what you may lose by *not* taking the steps you have chosen in these four areas. In other words, what price will you pay in the long run for neglecting to take these four steps toward greater vitality and health?

What I have to lose is _____

_____

_____

_____

Now in light of the same consideration, write down what the *benefits* to your life will be if you *do* take these four steps toward greater vitality and health.

What I have to gain is _____

_____

_____

_____

Now make a declaration of your commitment to these four steps in the light of what you have seen through this consideration. ____

_____

_____

_____

_____

Your Wellness Journal

Having committed to taking one concrete step in each of the four areas, look ahead and see where you would like to be in six months. Outline a process of additional steps in each of these areas. Again, be realistic. If you begin by meditating ten minutes each morning, don't plan to be meditating two hours a day in six months. You may well be doing just that. But don't burden yourself in advance with a stress-inducing commitment. Each step should be challenging but not overwhelming. And a three-week cycle in each step should be completed before going on to the next step.

After considering in detail what you would like to be doing in each of the four areas six months from now, write a journal entry to yourself *as if* the six months have already passed and you have attained your goals. Vividly feel and see yourself as you describe yourself in this entry. Experience the changes and the accomplishment of your goals in your imagination. This is a virtual reality experiment in which you anchor your vision of your future self in the present. Below, I give an example of my own journal entry.

WELLNESS JOURNAL, JANUARY 1, 2000

What a wonderful process I've had these past six months. I began with my five healthy salads per week. After three weeks, I cut all junk food out of my diet (except for my monthly ice-cream treat). The last four months I've been reducing my meal portions, adding fruit snacks, and generally tinkering with and improving my eating habits. And I've lost twenty pounds—my six-month goal. My friends tell me I look ten years younger, too.

My exercising has something to do with that. I started my program of five 15-minute walks a week, and after one month,

I graduated to five twenty-five-to-thirty-minute walks a week. At the end of two months, my body felt so limber and energized that I signed up for dance class two nights a week. Since then, it's been three walks and two dance classes a week, and I'm ready for John Travolta! My energy level has doubled, and I haven't gotten any colds or flus this season. My immune system is in top shape.

My new diet and exercise program has boosted my immune system to a whole new level. And my stillness practice has definitely had noticeable effects. I began with two five-minute periods of silence a day, morning and evening. I played around with different methods for the first couple of weeks to see what felt right. And I increased to two ten-minute periods at the end of the first month. I've created a program that I now follow. I begin with two minutes of breathing. Then I enter the Mindshift state, say a healing prayer/affirmation, and visualize brilliant white light filling my body, saturating every cell, and energizing me on every level. I do this for a minute or two, then meditate for the remainder of each period. I'm now up to two half-hour stillness/meditation periods per day, which feels like all that I need.

I feel so much clearer, and I notice there is a calm center in me that I can access in the midst of the busiest days. I am more present with others, and things that used to irritate me don't have the same force they used to. I see them coming and release them before they get to me. And my intuition is more active then ever. Insights come with a new kind of flow in relation to concerns, relationships, and projects. I'm more sensitive to the subtle signals of my own body/mind than ever, and sensitive to the emotional and physical condition of others. I feel I am on the path of radiant health and life.

And I'm having so much fun just being alive. I made a commitment in the beginning that I would laugh, and make at least one other person laugh, every day—even if I had to call someone up and tell him or her a joke. And a few times I have. But I can feel that laughter does heal and energize. It's not only better than champagne; it's the fountain of youth!

So I lift a glass of the sparkling water of life to salute my inner physician, who guides me like an old and intimate friend

on this exhilarating journey. And I offer a toast: "*L'Chayim!*
to life!"

After you've written in your journal, make a copy of your entry and
put it up where you can see it—on your desk at work, on your
refrigerator, or on your bulletin board. Choose a specific time once
each week to read it in the Mindshift state. Each time you do this,
re-experience your future self in your imagination, and recommit to
your vision. And meanwhile, keep taking those steps!

Let me share one of my steps, which is reading this poem by Margery
Johnson several times a week. This inspiring poem is a reminder of
my healing journey.

YOU ARE

You are wiser than you know, more courageous than you guess.
You are stronger than you feel in the greatness of your soul.
You are younger than your years; you are beautiful to see.
You can hold your joy complete underneath emotion's tears.
You are loved beyond your dreams, far more special than you
    think.
You are one with the Divine. Life is kinder than it seems.
Child of God, accept that love caring, singing through your mind.
Every miracle is yours. You are wonderful. **Believe**!

Multilevel Stress Busters

Let us end this chapter with a list of Stress Busters, things you can
do proactively to maintain your equilibrium in the midst of your
busy life, and heal stress as or even before it occurs. These are practical, commonsense keys to a life of radiant health.

- Adequate break time—establish regular periods in the day or
  random moments in which you *stop, relax, release, center, and
  rejuvenate* your body/mind.
- Slow down by focusing on one thing at a time. Let yourself be
  fully present to whatever you are doing and whomever you are
  with.

- Take a catnap whenever possible. Winston Churchill said that his daily naps gave him the stamina to endure the crisis of leading his nation through World War II. Thomas Edison also napped religiously, as did Napoleon. (Though perhaps he missed a crucial nap, just before the battle at Waterloo.)
- Take every opportunity to be in nature. Nature heals. Walk in a garden, park, or natural preserve. Look up at the sky. Enjoy the clouds. Soak up the sun.
- Smile and laugh every chance you get. Smiles and laughter infuse your body with healing chemistry and lighten your mood and that of others.
- Have faith in something, at least in yourself. Faith moves mountains.
- Remind yourself every day that you are a special part of a great universal plan; that you are in this body to perform a task that only you can do; that you are as important as every other human being; and the world would not be the same without you.
- Do something for others. Under stress, we tend to focus too much on our situation and ourselves. But often the best remedy is to focus on someone else. Be a Good Samaritan to someone in need—the joy you give others may heal you both.
- Adopt a credo that gives your life meaning, and make it an attitude and a habit. It can be a one-word reminder, such as "kindness" or "generosity"; or a line from a poem, affirmation, or prayer, such as "As I embrace life, life embraces me."
- Read something inspirational every day.
- Have a dream, a vision, and an inspiring goal. And take at least one small step each day to make it come true. Remember: "Hold fast to dreams, for if dreams die, life is a broken winged bird that cannot fly."
- Practice listening to others. Listening is an uncommon skill that will take you a very long way in life.
- Apologize, if an apology is in order. It will make you, and others, feel better.
- Ventilate—express your feelings. Holding in or suppressing your emotions is not a virtue. This doesn't mean yell at others when you are in a bad mood. But a good cry or a straightforward statement about your feelings is healthy for everyone.
- Practice detachment by seeing the Big Picture, the long-term

arc in which this moment is only that—a moment. Learn to step outside difficult situations by shifting your perspective.

- Practice forgiveness at every opportunity.
- Assume responsibility for your feelings. Don't credit or blame others for making you feel angry, happy, sad, or irritated.
- Practice enjoying waiting in lines and even driving in rush-hour traffic.
- Take time to celebrate how wonderful life really is.

PRACTICE: BUSTING STRESS

Pick any two stress busters each week for three months. Observe any changes at the end of each week. What have you noticed? ____

_____

_____

An ending always signals a beginning. So the ending of this book represents a new beginning for you and for me. I leave you with the apt and immortal words of Goethe: "Whatever you can do or dream you can, begin it. Boldness has genius, power, and magic in it. Begin it now."

ENDNOTES

Chapter 1. The Intuitive Voice Speaks

1. Marcia Emery and Jeffrey Mishlove, *Cultivating Intuition: Your Vehicle for Personal and Organizational Success*. Midwest Association of Humanistic Psychology (AHP) Conference, Indianapolis, Indiana, March 1995.

Chapter 3. Optimal Health Is an Inside Job

1. Deepak Chopra, *Creating Health: How to Wake Up the Body's Intelligence*. Boston: Houghton Mifflin, 1991, pp. ix–x.

2. Bernie Siegel, *Love, Medicine, and Miracles*. New York: Harper & Row, 1986. *Peace, Love, and Healing*. New York: Harper & Row, 1989.

Chapter 4. The Healing Wisdom of the Dream

1. Patricia Garfield, *The Healing Power of Dreams*. New York: Simon & Schuster, 1991, p. 17.

2. Bernie Siegel, *Love, Medicine, and Miracles*. New York: Harper & Row, 1986, pp. 113–14.

3. Robert Van de Castle, *Our Dreaming Mind*. New York: Ballantine Books, 1994, p. 438.

4. Van de Castle, *Our Dreaming Mind*, pp. 436–37.

Chapter 6. The Proactive Posture for Maintaining Perfect Health

1. Gerald Epstein, *Healing Visualization: Creating Health Through Imagery*. New York: Bantam Books, 1990, p. 200.

Chapter 10. Calling the Hotline for Another Person

1. Henry Reed, *Exercise Your Intuitive Heart: Discover All Your Heart Knows*. Mouth of Wilson, VA: Hermes Home Press, 1997, pp. 30–38.

2. Larry Dossey, *Healing Words: The Power of Prayer and the Practice of Medicine*. New York: HarperCollins, 1993, pp. 169–85.

3. Dossey, *Healing Words*, pp. 179–85.

RESOURCES

A GUIDE TO PEOPLE MENTIONED IN THE BOOK

D. Lawrence Burk, Jr., M.D.
Associate Professor of Radiology
Director of Integrative Medicine Education
Duke University Medical Center
Box 3808
Durham, NC 27710
919-684-1990
fax: 919-684-7137
beeper: 919-970-6589

Norma B. De Armon
Silva Mind and Creative Visualization
920 Ramona Avenue
Albany, CA 94706

Marcia Emery, Ph.D.
1502 Tenth Street
Berkeley, CA 94710
510-526-5510
fax: 510-526-9555
PowerHunch@aol.com
http://members.aol.com/PowerHunch

Jill Gregory
Dream Library and Archive
P.O. Box 866
Novato, CA 94948
415-897-7955

Bingkun Hu, Ph.D.
2114 Sacramento Street
Berkeley, CA 94702
510-841-6810

Karen Kramer, Ph.D.
1314 Ordway Street
Berkeley, CA 94702
510-527-7154
fax: 510-527-8373
Karen_Kramer@compuserve.com
www.healthyspirit.com

Gladys McGarey, M.D.
7350 East Stetson, Suite 204
Scottsdale, AZ 85251
602-990-1528

Caroline Myss, Ph.D.
7144 North Harlem Avenue #1305
Chicago, IL 60631
312-409-3071
http://www.myss.com

Belleruth Naparstek, LISW
Image Paths, Inc.
891 Moe Drive, Suite C
Akron, OH 44310
800-800-8661 fax: 330-633-3778
http://www.healthjourneys.com

Hanna Nathans
Fransen van de Puttelaan 34-36
3707 EH
Zeist, Netherlands
030-6931914
fax: 011-31 30 6921162

Sheba Penner
619-445-8371
fax: 619-445-1900

Henry Reed, Ph.D.
Hermes Home Press
3777 Fox Creek Road
Mouth of Wilson, VA 24363
1-800-398-1370
HenryReed@starbuck.net
www.starbuck.net

Ilana Rubenfeld
Rubenfeld Synergy Center
115 Waverly Place
New York, NY 10011
212-254-5100
fax: 212-254-1174
rubenfeld@aol.com
http://members.aol.com/rubenfeld/synergy/index.html

Meredith Sabini, Ph.D.
Licensed Psychologist
MCEP Provider
1670 University Avenue
Berkeley, CA 94703
510-845-1767

Jean Slane, M.D.
Wiselives Clinic
8320 West Bluemound Road, Suite 125
Wauwatosa, WI 53213
414-302-3800
fax: 414-302-3813

Patrick Tribble, D.C.
912 The Alameda
Berkeley, CA 94707
510-525-4825
fax: 510-525-4826

Robert Van de Castle, Ph.D.
2793 Barrsden Farm
Charlottesville, VA 22911
804-975-1980
RVDECASTLE@aol.com

Alan Vaughan, Ph.D.
1446 Yale #C
Santa Monica, CA 90404.
310-586-1535
fax: 310-586-1585
e-mail: AlanPsy@aol.com

BOOKS

Achterberg, Jeanne. (1985) *Imagery in Healing*. Boston: Shambhala.

Adrienne, Carol. (1998) *The Purpose of Your Life*. New York: Eagle Brook.

Agor, Weston. (1989) *Intuition in Organizations*. Newbury Park, CA: Sage.

————. (1984) *Intuitive Management*. Englewood Cliffs, NJ: Prentice Hall.

————. (1986) *The Logic of Intuitive Decision Making*. New York: Quorum.

Arrien, Angeles. (1987) *The Tarot Handbook*. Sonoma, CA: Arcus.

————. (1993) *The 4 Fold Way: Walking the Paths of the Warrior, Teacher, Healer, and Visionary*. New York: HarperCollins.

Beasley, Victor. (1995) *Intuition by Design*. Blue Hill, ME: Medicine Bear Publishing.

Berger, Ruth. (1995) *Medical Intuition: How to Combine Inner Resources with Modern Medicine*. York Beach, ME: Samuel Weiser.

Borysenko, Joan. (1993) *Fire in the Soul*. New York: Warner.

Borysenko, Joan, and Miroslav Borysenko. (1994) *The Power of the Mind to Heal*. Carson, CA: Hay House.

Chopra, Deepak. (1993) *Ageless Body, Timeless Mind*. New York: Harmony Books.

———. (1991) *Creating Health*. Boston: Houghton Mifflin.

———. (1990) *Quantum Healing*. New York: Bantam.

Choquette, Sonia. (1997) *Your Heart's Desire*. New York: Three Rivers Press.

Contino, Richard. (1996) *Trust Your Gut!* New York: American Management Association.

Csikszentmihalyi, Mihaly. (1990) *Flow: The Psychology of Optimal Experiences*. New York: HarperPerennial.

Davis-Floyd, Robbie, and Sven P. Arvidson. (1997) *Intuition: The Inside Story*. New York: Routledge.

Day, Laura. (1996) *Practical Intuition*. New York: Villard.

———. (1997) *Practical Intuition for Business*. New York: HarperCollins.

Dean, Douglas, et al. (1974) *Executive ESP*. Englewood Cliffs, NJ: Prentice Hall.

Dossey, Larry, M.D. (1993) *Healing Words*. San Francisco: HarperSanFrancisco.

Einstein, Patricia. (1997) *Intuition: The Path to Inner Wisdom*. Rockport, MA: Element.

Emery, Marcia. (1994) *Dr. Marcia Emery's Intuition Workbook: An Expert's Guide to Unlocking the Wisdom of Your Subconscious Mind*. Englewood Cliffs, NJ: Prentice Hall.

Epstein, Gerald. (1990) *Healing Visualization: Creating Health Through Imagery*. New York: Bantam.

Feinstein, David, and Stanley Krippner. (1997) *The Mythic Path*. New York: Tarcher/Putnam.

Frantz, Roger, and Alex N. Pattakos, eds. (1996) *Intuition at Work*. San Francisco: New Leaders.

Franquemont, Sharon. (1997) *Do It Yourself Intuition*. Oakland, CA: Intuition Enterprises.

———. (1999) *You Already Know What to Do*. New York: Tarcher/Putnam.

Fuller, R. Buckminster. (1983) *Intuition*. San Luis Obispo, CA: Impact.

Garfield, Patricia. (1992) *The Healing Power of Dreams*. New York: Fireside.

Goldberg, Philip. (1983) *The Intuitive Edge*. Los Angeles: Tarcher.

Hendricks, Gay, and Kate Ludeman. (1996) *The Corporate Mystic*. New York: Bantam.

Kautz, William H., and Melanie Branon. (1989) *Intuiting the Future: A New Age Vision of the 1990s*. San Francisco: Harper & Row.

Knaster, Mirka. (1996) *Discovering the Body's Wisdom*. New York: Bantam.

Miller, Emmett. (1997) *Deep Healing*. Carlsbad, CA: Hay House.

Miller, Marlane. (1997) *Brainstyles: Change Your Life Without Changing Who You Are*. New York: Simon & Schuster.

Millman, Dan. (1998) *Everyday Enlightenment: The Twelve Gateways to Personal Growth*. New York: Warner.

Mishlove, Jeffrey. (1992) *Thinking Allowed*. Tulsa, OK: Council Oak Books.

———. (1997) *Roots of Consciousness*. New York: Marlow.

Munn, Michael. (1998) *Beyond Business as Usual*. Boston: Butterworth-Heinemann.

Myss, Caroline. (1996) *Anatomy of the Spirit*. New York: Harmony Books.

———. (1997) *Why People Don't Heal and How They Can*. New York: Harmony Books.

Myss, Caroline, and C. Norman Shealy. (1988) *Creation of Health: The Emotional, Psychological, and Spiritual Responses That Promote Health and Healing*. Walpole, NH: Stillpoint.

Nadell, L., with J. Haims and R. Stempson. (1990) *Sixth Sense*. New York: Prentice-Hall.

Naparstek, Belleruth. (1997) *Your Sixth Sense: Activating Your Psychic Potential*. New York: HarperCollins.

Northrup, Christiane. (1994) *Women's Bodies, Women's Wisdom*. New York: Bantam.

Ornish, Dean. (1990) *Dr. Dean Ornish's Program for Reversing Heart Disease*. New York: Random House.

Palmer, Wendy. (1994) *The Intuitive Body*. Berkeley, CA: North Atlantic Books.

Parikh, Jagdish. (1994) *Intuition: The New Frontier of Management*. Cambridge, MA: Blackwell.

Pehrson, Mark B., and Susan Mehrtens. (1997) *Intuitive Imagery: A Resource at Work*. Boston: Butterworth-Heinemann.

Peirce, Penney. (1998) *The Intuitive Way: A Guide to Living from Inner Wisdom*. Hillsboro, OR: Beyond Words Publishing.

Pert, Candace B. (1997) *Molecules of Emotion: Why You Feel the Way You Feel*. New York: Scribner.

Ray, Michael, and Rochelle Myers. (1986) *Creativity in Business*. New York: Doubleday.

Reed, Henry. (1991) *Dream Solutions*. San Rafael, CA: New World Library.

———. (1997) *Exercise Your Intuitive Heart: Discover All Your Heart Knows*. Mouth of Wilson, VA: Hermes Home Press.

———. (1989) *Getting Help from Your Dreams*. New York: Ballantine.

Remen, Rachel. (1996) *Kitchen Table Wisdom*. New York: Riverhead Books.

Robinson, Lynn. (1994) *Coming out of Your Psychic Closet: How to Unlock Your Naturally Intuitive Self*. Mobile, AL: Factor Press.

Rosanoff, Nancy (1988) *Intuition Workout*. Boulder Creek, CA: Aslan Publishing.

Rowan, Roy. (1986) *The Intuitive Manager*. Boston: Little, Brown.

Ryback, David. (1998) *Putting Emotional Intelligence to Work*. Boston: Butterworth-Heinemann.

Salk, Jonas. (1983) *Anatomy of Reality: Merging of Intuition and Reason*. New York: Columbia University Press.

Schulz, Mona Lisa. (1998) *Awakening Intuition*. New York: Harmony Books.

Schulz, Ron. (1994) *Unconventional Wisdom*. New York: HarperBusiness.

Shallcross, Doris J., and Dorothy Sisk. (1989) *Intuition: An Inner Way of Knowing*. Buffalo, NY: Bearly Limited.

Shealy, Norman, M.D., and Caroline Myss. (1988) *The Creation of Health*. Walpole, NH: Stillpoint.

Siegel, Bernie, M.D. (1986) *Love, Medicine, and Miracles*. New York: Harper & Row.

Siegel, Bernie. (1989) *Peace, Love, and Healing.* New York: Harper & Row.

Taggart, Bill. (1994) *Accessing Intuition: A Research Bibliography.* Available at www.The-Intuitive-Self.com.

Tower, Virginia B. (1987) *The Process of Intuition.* Wheaton, IL: Theosophical Publishers.

Trowbridge, Robert. (1996) *The Hidden Meaning of Illness—Disease as a Symbol and Metaphor.* Virginia Beach, VA: A.R.E. Press.

Vaughan, Alan. (1998) *Doorways to Higher Consciousness.* Williamsburg, VA: Celest Press.

———. (1982) *The Edge of Tomorrow.* New York: Coward, McCann.

———. (1973) *Patterns of Prophecy.* New York: Hawthorn.

———. (1991) *Power of Positive Prophecy.* New York: Aquarian Press.

Vaughan, Frances E. (1979) *Awakening Intuition.* Garden City, NY: Anchor Books.

Weintraub, Sandra. (1998) *The Hidden Intelligence: Innovation Through Intuition.* Boston: Butterworth-Heinemann.

Windsor, Joan. (1987) *Dreams and Healing.* New York: Dodd, Mead.

AUDIOCASSETTES

Emery, Marcia. (1995) *Intuition: How to Use Your Gut Instinct for Greater Personal Power.* Six audiotapes. Nightingale Conant. 800-323-5552.

———. (1996) *Intuition: How to Use Your Gut Instinct for Greater Personal Power.* Two audiotapes. Simon & Schuster.

Experiential Seminars with Mikel. The Mikel Institute. 612-546-7902.

Franquemont, Sharon. (1999) *Intuition: The Electric Self.* Sounds True. 800-333-5766.

Goldberg, Philip. (1987) *Unlocking Your Intuition.* Audio Renaissance Tapes.

Levey, Joel, and Michelle Levey. (1993) *The Focused Mind State.* Nightingale Conant. 800-323-5552.

Li Sung Speaks (Alan Vaughan, Channel). Audiotape series. L & L Management (see below).

Millman, Dan. (1995) *Practical Wisdom.* Books Now. 800-266-5766.

Myss, Caroline. *Energy Anatomy and Spiritual Madness.* Sounds True. 800-333-9185.

Naparstek, Belleruth. *Health Journeys: For People Working on Their Relationship* (1994); *For General Wellness* (1994); *For People Experiencing Stress* (1995). New York: Time-Warner Audio Books.

———. (1997) *Your Sixth Sense: Activating Your Psychic Potential.* HarperAudio.

Palmer, Helen. (1993) *Intuition Training.* Shambala Publications.

Robinson, Winter. (1995) *Discovering Intuition.* Buxton, ME: Tor Down.

Rosanoff, Nancy. (1996) *Use Your Intuition.* Nancy Rosanoff & Associates. 914-769-7226.

Van de Castle, Robert. (1989) *Psychic Dreaming.* Renaissance Tapes.

Vaughan, Alan. *The Path of Channeling and the Path of Healing.* L & L Management (see below).

VIDEOCASSETTES

Adler, Ray. (1996) *Improve Your Intuition.* Alder Media Production. 609-822-5423.

Global Intuition Network, Producer. (1992) *The Role of Intuition in Decision Making.* 915-747-5227.

Martin, Sandra, Producer. (1997) *Intuition: The Spark That Ignites.* Paraview. 212-489-5343.

Myss, Caroline, and C. Norman Shealy. *Vision, Creativity, and Intuition.* Phone/fax 417-467-3102.

Myss, Caroline. (1997) *The Energetics of Healing.* 800-333-9185.

Weston, Victoria, Producer. (1997) *The Intuitive Factor: Genius or Chance?* 404-876-7149.

INTUITION RESOURCES

Jeffrey Mishlove, Ph.D., President
Intuition Network
369-B Third Street #161
San Rafael, CA 94901
415-256-1137
fax: 415-456-2532
intuition.network@intuition.org
www.intuition.org

Intuition Magazine
275 Brannan, third floor
San Francisco, CA 94107
415-538-8171
fax: 415-538-8175

RELATED ORGANIZATIONS

Association of Humanistic Psychology (AHP)
45 Franklin Street, Suite 315
San Francisco, CA 94102
415-864-8850
fax: 415-864-8853
Ahpoffice@aol.com

Association for Study of Dreams (ASD)
P.O. Box 1600
Vienna, VA 22183
703-242-0062
ASDreams@aol.com
www.outreach.org/gmcc/asd/

Bay Area Dream Group (BADG)
Eric Snyder
1325 Barlow Lane
Sebastopol, CA 95472
707-824-9121

Institute of Noetic Sciences (IONS)
475 Gate Five Road, Suite 300
Sausalito, CA 94965-0909
415-331-5650
fax: 415-331-5673

Leland R. Kaiser, Ph.D., Director
Kaiser Institute
P.O. Box 339
Brighton, CO 80601
303-659-8815
www.Kaiser.net

SOURCES FOR AUDIOCASSETTES

Intuitive Problem Solving, Exploring Your Dreams, Precognitive Dreams by Marcia Emery, Ph.D; and *Ocean View Mountain Trail—A Meditation* by James D. Emery, M.M., are available from
Intuitive Management Consulting Corporation (IMCC)
1502 Tenth Street
Berkeley, CA 94710
510-526-5510
fax: 510-526-9555
PowerHunch@aol.com

ABOUT THE AUTHOR

Marcia Emery, Ph.D., is a noted psychologist, consultant, college professor, international lecturer, and author who has been teaching people how to cultivate their intuition for decades. Her clinical, academic, and business background give her rare insight into the phenomenon of intuition and its practical application.

She has presented her acclaimed intuitive power seminars to scores of individuals from many leading organizations, including Lucent Technologies (formerly AT&T), Amway Corporation, Blue Care Network, General Motors, Donnelly Corporation, Herman Miller Company, Hewlett Packard, Butterworth Hospital, Michigan Employment Security Commission, and Steelcase. Through her written publications, speaking engagements, numerous television and radio appearances, and seminars, Dr. Emery has contributed greatly to the public's interest in intuition. She is the author of *Dr. Marcia Emery's Intuition Workbook: An Expert's Guide to Unlocking the Wisdom of Your Subconscious Mind* as well as a six-cassette Nightingale-Conant audiotape series called *Intuition: How to Use Your Gut Instinct for Greater Personal Power.*

Dr. Emery is the director of education for the Intuition Network. With her husband, James D. Emery, she is currently setting up local intuition study groups throughout the United States and abroad.